EARLY CHILDHOOD EDUCATION SERIES
Sharon Ryan, Editor

ADVISORY BOARD: Celia Genishi, Doris Fromberg, Carrie Lobman, Rachel Theilheimer, Dominic Gullo, Amita Gupta, Beatrice Fennimore, Sue Grieshaber, Jackie Marsh, Mindy Blaise, Gail Yuen, Alice Honig, Betty Jones, Stephanie Feeney, Stacie Goffin, Beth Graue

Seen and Heard: Children's Rights in Early Childhood Education
ELLEN LYNN HALL & JENNIFER KOFKIN RUDKIN

Young Investigators: The Project Approach in the Early Years, 2nd Ed.
JUDY HARRIS HELM & LILIAN G. KATZ

Supporting Boys' Learning: Strategies for Teacher Practice, PreK–Grade 3
BARBARA SPRUNG, MERLE FROSCHL, & NANCY GROPPER

Young English Language Learners: Current Research and Emerging Directions for Practice and Policy
EUGENE E. GARCÍA & ELLEN C. FREDE, EDS.

Connecting Emergent Curriculum and Standards in the Early Childhood Classroom: Strengthening Content and Teacher Practice
SYDNEY L. SCHWARTZ & SHERRY M. COPELAND

Infants and Toddlers at Work: Using Reggio-Inspired Materials to Support Brain Development
ANN LEWIN-BENHAM

The View from the Little Chair in the Corner: Improving Teacher Practice and Early Childhood Learning (Wisdom from an Experienced Classroom Observer)
CINDY RZASA BESS

Culture and Child Development in Early Childhood Programs: Practices for Quality Education and Care
CAROLLEE HOWES

The Early Intervention Guidebook for Families and Professionals: Partnering for Success
BONNIE KEILTY

The Story in the Picture: Inquiry and Artmaking with Young Children
CHRISTINE MULCAHEY

Educating and Caring for Very Young Children: The Infant/Toddler Curriculum, 2nd Ed.
DORIS BERGEN, REBECCA REID, & LOUIS TORELLI

Beginning School: U.S. Policies in International Perspective
RICHARD M. CLIFFORD & GISELE M. CRAWFORD, EDS.

Emergent Curriculum in the Primary Classroom: Interpreting the Reggio Emilia Approach in Schools
CAROL ANNE WIEN, ED.

Enthusiastic and Engaged Learners: Approaches to Learning in the Early Childhood Classroom
MARILOU HYSON

Powerful Children: Understanding How to Teach and Learn Using the Reggio Approach
ANN LEWIN-BENHAM

The Early Care and Education Teaching Workforce at the Fulcrum: An Agenda for Reform
SHARON LYNN KAGAN, KRISTIE KAUERZ, & KATE TARRANT

Windows on Learning: Documenting Young Children's Work, 2nd Ed.
JUDY HARRIS HELM, SALLEE BENEKE, & KATHY STEINHEIMER

Ready or Not: Leadership Choices in Early Care and Education
STACIE G. GOFFIN & VALORA WASHINGTON

Supervision in Early Childhood Education: A Developmental Perspective, 3rd Ed.
JOSEPH J. CARUSO WITH M. TEMPLE FAWCETT

Guiding Children's Behavior: Developmental Discipline in the Classroom
EILEEN S. FLICKER & JANET ANDRON HOFFMAN

What If All the Kids Are White? Anti-Bias Multicultural Education with Young Children and Families
LOUISE DERMAN-SPARKS & PATRICIA G. RAMSEY

The War Play Dilemma: What Every Parent and Teacher Needs to Know, 2nd Ed.
DIANE E. LEVIN & NANCY CARLSSON-PAIGE

Possible Schools: The Reggio Approach to Urban Education
ANN LEWIN-BENHAM

Everyday Goodbyes: Starting School and Early Care– A Guide to the Separation Process
NANCY BALABAN

Playing to Get Smart
ELIZABETH JONES & RENATTA M. COOPER

How to Work with Standards in the Early Childhood Classroom
CAROL SEEFELDT

In the Spirit of the Studio: Learning from the Atelier of Reggio Emilia
LELLA GANDINI, LYNN T. HILL, LOUISE BOYD CADWELL, & CHARLES SCHWALL, EDS.

Understanding Assessment and Evaluation in Early Childhood Education, 2nd Ed.
DOMINIC F. GULLO

Negotiating Standards in the Primary Classroom: The Teacher's Dilemma
CAROL ANNE WIEN

Teaching and Learning in a Diverse World: Multicultural Education for Young Children, 3rd Ed.
PATRICIA G. RAMSEY

The Emotional Development of Young Children: Building an Emotion-Centered Curriculum, 2nd Ed.
MARILOU HYSON

Effective Partnering for School Change: Improving Early Childhood Education in Urban Classrooms
JIE-QI CHEN & PATRICIA HORSCH WITH KAREN DeMOSS & SUZANNE L. WAGNER

Let's Be Friends: Peer Competence and Social Inclusion in Early Childhood Programs
KRISTEN MARY KEMPLE

Young Children Continue to Reinvent Arithmetic– 2nd Grade, 2nd Ed.
CONSTANCE KAMII

Major Trends and Issues in Early Childhood Education: Challenges, Controversies, and Insights, 2nd Ed.
JOAN PACKER ISENBERG & MARY RENCK JALONGO, EDS.

The Power of Projects: Meeting Contemporary Challenges in Early Childhood Classrooms– Strategies and Solutions
JUDY HARRIS HELM & SALLEE BENEKE, EDS.

Bringing Learning to Life: The Reggio Approach to Early Childhood Education
LOUISE BOYD CADWELL

(continued)

W9-BGK-177

Early Childhood Education Series titles, continued

The Colors of Learning: Integrating the Visual Arts into the Early Childhood Curriculum
ROSEMARY ALTHOUSE, MARGARET H. JOHNSON, & SHARON T. MITCHELL

A Matter of Trust: Connecting Teachers and Learners in the Early Childhood Classroom
CAROLLEE HOWES & SHARON RITCHIE

Widening the Circle: Including Children with Disabilities in Preschool Programs
SAMUEL L. ODOM, ED.

Children with Special Needs: Lessons for Early Childhood Professionals
MARJORIE J. KOSTELNIK, ESTHER ETSUKO ONAGA, BARBARA ROHDE, & ALICE PHIPPS WHIREN

Developing Constructivist Early Childhood Curriculum: Practical Principles and Activities
RHETA DEVRIES, BETTY ZAN, CAROLYN HILDEBRANDT, REBECCA EDMIASTON, & CHRISTINA SALES

Outdoor Play: Teaching Strategies with Young Children
JANE PERRY

Embracing Identities in Early Childhood Education: Diversity and Possibilities
SUSAN GRIESHABER & GAILE S. CANNELLA, EDS.

Bambini: The Italian Approach to Infant/Toddler Care
LELLA GANDINI & CAROLYN POPE EDWARDS, EDS.

Serious Players in the Primary Classroom, 2nd Ed.
SELMA WASSERMANN

Telling a Different Story
CATHERINE WILSON

Young Children Reinvent Arithmetic: Implications of Piaget's Theory, 2nd Ed.
CONSTANCE KAMII

Managing Quality in Young Children's Programs
MARY L. CULKIN, ED.

The Early Childhood Curriculum, 3rd Ed.
CAROL SEEFELDT, ED.

Leadership in Early Childhood, 2nd Ed.
JILLIAN RODD

Inside a Head Start Center
DEBORAH CEGLOWSKI

Bringing Reggio Emilia Home
LOUISE BOYD CADWELL

Master Players
GRETCHEN REYNOLDS & ELIZABETH JONES

Understanding Young Children's Behavior
JILLIAN RODD

Understanding Quantitative and Qualitative Research in Early Childhood Education
WILLIAM L. GOODWIN & LAURA D. GOODWIN

Diversity in the Classroom, 2nd Ed.
FRANCES E. KENDALL

Developmentally Appropriate Practice in "Real Life"
CAROL ANNE WIEN

Experimenting with the World
HARRIET K. CUFFARO

Quality in Family Child Care and Relative Care
SUSAN KONTOS, CAROLLEE HOWES, MARYBETH SHINN, & ELLEN GALINSKY

Using the Supportive Play Model
MARGARET K. SHERIDAN, GILBERT M. FOLEY, & SARA H. RADLINSKI

The Full-Day Kindergarten, 2nd Ed.
DORIS PRONIN FROMBERG

Assessment Methods for Infants and Toddlers
DORIS BERGEN

Young Children Continue to Reinvent Arithmetic—3rd Grade: Implications of Piaget's Theory
CONSTANCE KAMII WITH SALLY JONES LIVINGSTON

Moral Classrooms, Moral Children
RHETA DEVRIES & BETTY ZAN

Diversity and Developmentally Appropriate Practices
BRUCE L. MALLORY & REBECCA S. NEW, EDS.

Changing Teaching, Changing Schools
FRANCES O'CONNELL RUST

Physical Knowledge in Preschool Education
CONSTANCE KAMII & RHETA DEVRIES

Ways of Assessing Children and Curriculum
CELIA GENISHI, ED.

The Play's the Thing
ELIZABETH JONES & GRETCHEN REYNOLDS

Scenes from Day Care
ELIZABETH BALLIETT PLATT

Making Friends in School
PATRICIA G. RAMSEY

The Whole Language Kindergarten
SHIRLEY RAINES & ROBERT CANADY

Multiple Worlds of Child Writers
ANNE HAAS DYSON

The Good Preschool Teacher
WILLIAM AYERS

The Piaget Handbook for Teachers and Parents
ROSEMARY PETERSON & VICTORIA FELTON-COLLINS

Visions of Childhood
JOHN CLEVERLEY & D. C. PHILLIPS

Ideas Influencing Early Childhood Education
EVELYN WEBER

The Joy of Movement in Early Childhood
SANDRA R. CURTIS

Seen *and* Heard
Children's Rights in Early Childhood Education

ELLEN LYNN HALL
JENNIFER KOFKIN RUDKIN

Foreword by Bonnie Neugebauer

The Althouse Press
The University of Western Ontario
London, Ontario

Teachers College
Columbia University
New York and London

Published simultaneously by Teachers College Press, 1234 Amsterdam Avenue, New York, NY 10027 and The Althouse Press, The Faculty of Education, The University of Western Ontario, 1137 Western Road, London, Ontario, Canada N6G 1G7.

All photos courtesy of the Boulder Journey School.

Library of Congress Cataloging-in-Publication Data

Hall, Ellen Lynn.
Seen and heard: children's rights in early childhood education / Ellen Lynn Hall, Jennifer Kofkin Rudkin.
   p.   cm.
   Includes bibliographical references and index.
   ISBN 978-0-8077-5160-2 (pbk.)—ISBN 978-0-8077-5161-9 (hardcover)
1. Reggio Emilia approach (Early childhood education)—Colorado—Boulder. 2. Children's rights—Colorado—Boulder. 3. Early childhood education—Colorado—Boulder. I. Rudkin, Jennifer Kofkin. II. Title.
LB1029.R35H35 2010
323.3'520978863—dc22   2010032729

Library and Archives Canada Cataloguing in Publication

Hall, Ellen Lynn
   Seen and heard : children's rights in early childhood education / Ellen Lynn Hall, Jennifer Kofkin Rudkin.

Co-published by Teachers College Press.
Includes bibliographical references and index.
ISBN 978-0-920354-72-8

   1. Reggio Emilia approach (Early childhood education).   2. Children's rights.   3. Early childhood education. I. Rudkin, Jennifer Kofkin II. Title.

LB1029.R35.H35 2010   323.3'52   C2010-907582-X

ISBN 978-0-8077-5160-2 (U.S. paperback)
ISBN 978-0-8077-5161-9 (U.S. hardcover)
ISBN 978-0-920354-72-8 (Canada paperback)

Printed on acid-free paper
Manufactured in the United States of America

18   17   16   15   14   13   12   11   8   7   6   5   4   3   2   1

To the children, families, and faculty of Boulder Journey School, whose strong and powerful voices, images, and work fill the pages of this book.

To the educators in the infant–toddler centers and preschools of Reggio Emilia, Italy, and to colleagues at Reggio Children who have inspired, encouraged, and supported our thinking about children's rights.

To people worldwide, who advocate for children's right to participation as citizens of the present and of the future.

To our children and grandchildren, with our deep love, respect, and gratitude.

Contents

Foreword *by Bonnie Neugebauer*   ix

Introduction   1

1 Tuning Adult Ears to the Voices of Young Children   7
Listening to Young Children   10
Children's Insights About Children's Rights   17
Conclusion   18

2 Children's Rights in the United States:
   Learning from the Social Movements of the 1960s   20
Children's Rights and New Conversations: In Praise of Stuttering   20
Dynamics of Oppression: "Our Similarities Are Different"   23
Conclusion   34

3 The Special Estate of Children's Rights:
   A Movement Like No Other   36
Balancing Protection and Participation   37
The Unique Status of Children   40
Conclusion   48

4 Children as Community Protagonists   50
The Social Context of Children's Communal Responsibilities:
Parents, Teachers, and Peers   52
The Role of Adults in Supporting Children as Community Protagonists:
Stepping In and Stepping Out   55
Valuing Conflict   58
Children as Protagonists in Global (as Well as Local) Communities   62
Conclusion   65

5 Children's Exploration of Rights
   Through the Construction of a Hamster City   68
A City for Crystal   68
The Importance of Movement   74
Balancing Protection and Participation   82

The Right to Community—To Care and Be Cared For 86
Conclusion 91

6 Children's Places **94**
A Fort of One's Own 94
Characteristics of Children's Places 96
Conclusion 109

Conclusion **112**

References **117**

Index **127**

About the Authors **133**

Foreword

Knowing, really believing, that children have rights is a huge responsibility. Understanding that all children have the same rights, regardless of their circumstances at birth, is a point of crisis for us as adults. Because if we really know this, what excuses can we possibly offer for the disparity of circumstances for children around the world?

Traditionally we think of rights as something bestowed, as if we hold the power to give these rights to children. This thinking provides a kind of safety net. If rights were ours to give, then there would be a way out of our responsibility—if the challenges are overwhelming, we can tell ourselves that we have done all that we can. But the mind shift to an understanding that children already have these rights, irrespective of our powers in play, means that all we can do is to honor these rights—or take them away.

What we feel about children's rights affects everything. It impacts how we are with children, what we offer, what we say, how we listen, the questions we ask, the opportunities we provide. It affects how we spend resources and what our priorities look like. We need to be clear about this. Believing in children's rights takes away the excuses, and our failures are laid bare for all to see. It's quite uncomfortable to have no way out of our obligations.

But in the same breath, if we do not give children their rights but rather know them to be birthrights, we do not bear sole responsibility for protecting these rights. Children themselves must be involved in using and safeguarding their rights. Our duty becomes that of enabling children to see and understand what their rights are—of exploring and learning, testing, questioning. Children need to own their rights and they need to understand the responsibilities that are embedded within them.

And then we must work together with children to protect these rights—empowering children to speak for themselves. Sometimes our best action is to get out of the way.

Through respectful and joyful explorations, Ellen Hall and Jennifer Rudkin have learned about rights with and from children. They have discovered how children understand rights and how rights issues impact life in a learning community. Through their work, they encourage all of us to do less speaking for children and more listening to what children have to share with us.

We have important work to do. Accepting our responsibilities to support the fundamental birthright of children gives us a new framework for being with children. *Seen and Heard: Children's Rights in Early Childhood Education* gives us the inspiration to see the possibilities for our journey.

—*Bonnie Neugebauer*

Introduction

This book summarizes research and theory as they pertain to young children's rights in the United States and illustrates key points through vivid stories and images collected at Boulder Journey School. Boulder Journey School is a school in Boulder, Colorado, where educators work alongside children aged 6 weeks to 6 years and their families. Since 1995, Boulder Journey School has studied the philosophy and pedagogy of the schools for young children in Reggio Emilia, Italy. Reggio Emilia's infant–toddler centers and preschools grew from community-run schools established largely by mothers in the wake of World War II. The threat of fascism convinced residents of the need to create schools that would encourage children to think and act for themselves. The early education schools of Reggio Emilia gained international attention in 1991 when a panel of experts commissioned by *Newsweek* magazine identified the schools for young children in Reggio Emilia as the best in the world (Municipality of Reggio Emilia Infant Toddler Centers and Preschools, 1999). Today, Reggio Emilia is a place of inspiration and collaboration for educators and researchers throughout the world dedicated to working with young children.

FOUNDATIONAL IDEAS

Three overlapping ideas are foundational to the Reggio Emilia approach, to Boulder Journey School, and to this book. The first is the notion of *the hundred languages of children*. Loris Malaguzzi, key architect of the Reggio Emilia approach to early childhood education, observed that young children participate in the world using "one hundred languages" for exploring, discovering, constructing, representing, and conveying their ideas.

> The child has a hundred languages
> A hundred hands
> A hundred thoughts
> A hundred ways of thinking (Edwards, Gandini, & Forman, 1998, p. 3)

In our culture, which often renders children invisible and silences young voices, it is important to honor the many ways in which children express themselves.

The second notion is the *pedagogy of listening*. Pedagogista Carlina Rinaldi has worked with educators in Reggio Emilia for over 40 years, "cultivating an attitude of 'learning' to learn (as John Dewey called it), an openness to change, and a willingness to discuss opposing points of view" (Filippini in Edwards et al., 1998, p. 130). Rinaldi speaks and writes eloquently about the importance of creating a context within which children and adults carefully attend to the world and to one another as they shape and reshape their questions and theories. In her words, "Very early in life, children demonstrate that they have a voice, but above all that they know how to listen and be listened to" (Rinaldi, 2001, p. 82).

The third essential idea, and the central tenet of this book, is that all children have the right to participate in the communities in which they reside, not as future citizens, but as citizens of the present. The idea that children have a right to participate in their communities gained unprecedented attention and legitimacy in 1989 when world leaders ratified the United Nations Convention on the Rights of the Child (UNCRC). The UNCRC was the first legally binding international instrument to recognize the civil, cultural, economic, political, and social rights of children. The UNCRC was a groundbreaking document for many reasons, not the least of which is its assertion that children have the right to participation, as well as protection and provision. Discourse on children's rights has long encompassed the need for adults to *provide* the resources necessary for children to survive and grow to their full potential, and the need for adults to *protect* children from harm, including abuse and exploitation. The UNCRC held that adults also have a responsibility to honor children's right to *participate* in family, cultural, and social life (UNICEF, n.d.).

The UNCRC inspired numerous articles, chapters, and books about children's rights. As a result, the collective sensitivity to children's rights has grown, although certainly there remains much distance to travel. The world community recently celebrated the 20th anniversary of the UNCRC, and so this is a fitting time to consider the enormous strides many have made on behalf of children and also to suggest directions for future growth.

DISTINCTIVE FOCUS

This book differs from existing books about children's rights in two important ways. First, this book focuses on *young* children's rights, whereas much of the literature on children's rights centers on the concerns of older children and adolescents, age groups where the line between childhood and adulthood blurs. The current discourse on children's rights often has ignored young children, for two reasons. First, adults tend to view infants, toddlers, and preschoolers as immature, dependent, and not yet fully formed, making the concept of rights irrelevant to them (e.g., Pugh & Selleck, 1996). Priscilla Alderson (2000b) noted a prevailing view of children as human *becomings* rather than human *beings*. A partial person could never be considered equal to a whole person, and so in this view children would not be entitled to the same rights as adults. An alternative view holds that children and adults are both human beings in the present, and also human becomings in that we all grow, learn, and change throughout our lives. A second reason why young children's rights have been neglected in the children's rights literature is that assessing the ideas of children, especially children who are not yet verbal, is challenging and requires novel approaches to research. Because educators at Boulder Journey School work with children as young as 6 weeks, we have tried to represent the voices of children beginning in infancy.

The second way in which this book differs from existing books is its commitment to considering young children's rights from the perspectives of the children themselves—a challenge that is even more notable given our focus on young children. Only a small subset of the growing literature on children's rights explores children's rights from children's perspectives (e.g., Cherney & Perry, 1996; S. Hart, Zeidner, & Pavlovic, 1996; Melton, 1980; Osler, 1998). Because a commitment to children's rights honors the voices of children, scholarship on this topic must include the children's own perspectives (Sommer, Pramling Samuelsson, & Hundeide, 2010). We believe that attentive listeners recognize wisdom in the communications of even the youngest children. Throughout this book we place children's words in a different font as a reminder to pay attention to their words, much in the way Georgia O'Keefe compelled people to recognize the beauty of small flowers by painting them on giant canvases. In addition, we attend to the "hundred" nonverbal languages in which children express themselves, by including painting, drawing, and photography. The book also includes many photographs of children at work and play. Thus, the pages of this book are very image-rich.

In this book, most of the images and stories that bring to life the scholarship on children's rights were collected at Boulder Journey School. The city of Boulder's population is 88% Caucasian, with an average household income above the national average (U.S. Census Bureau, 2008). Most of the children who appear in the pages that follow are fortunate in that they are not denied the rights to provision and protection. The authors would like to present our insights into children's right to participation, gleaned at Boulder Journey School, with respect for the plight of children and adults who are living and working in contexts permeated with violence, hunger, homelessness, and despair.

Although this book is centered within a school for young children and has particular relevance to teachers, administrators, and staff in educational contexts, we have tried to attend also to the perspectives of parents and other community members. Our hope is that this book's blend of scholarship and practice will appeal to students and practitioners in a variety of fields, as well as to all people who care about children.

OVERVIEW OF THIS BOOK

The book consists of six chapters that build on one another but also can be read as independent essays.

Chapter 1: The first chapter is an introduction to the general issues around children's rights and to the context in which these issues are explored, Boulder

Journey School. Children's rights are about adult ears as much as children's voices. This chapter offers advice to adults dedicated to listening to the voices of young children, such as the importance of honoring nonverbal communication and of adopting a patient attitude. A highlight of this chapter is a list of 61 rights generated by children at Boulder Journey School. This list is revisited throughout the book.

Chapter 2: This chapter is a consideration of the ways in which the struggle for children's rights parallels the struggles of earlier rights movements. This chapter compares and contrasts the children's rights movement with three other rights movements: Black civil rights, women's liberation, and disability rights. Issues explored include invisibility, disparities in size and strength, and the distinction between dependence and interdependence.

Chapter 3: While the previous chapter explored commonalities among the children's rights movement and other movements, this chapter takes the opposite approach, delineating what is unique about children's rights. It discusses the importance of (1) "child" as a status we all belong or have belonged to, (2) adult–child differences in bodies and minds, (3) differences in life experience, and (4) the unique love between adult and child.

Chapter 4: This chapter addresses the misconception that children focused on their own rights fail to develop a concern for others. We believe that respect for rights and assumption of social responsibility go hand in hand. We examine the role of adults in fostering children's citizenship, which includes respecting children's right to make their own decisions and the need for conflict.

Chapter 5: This chapter follows the thoughts and actions of a group of young children involved in a long-term project to build a city for their classroom hamster. As they consider how to create a just and beautiful world for Crystal the hamster, they uncover lessons with relevance to us all.

Chapter 6: The final chapter examines the importance of places children can claim as their own, where they can go alone or with other children. In these special places, children construct an understanding of their lives in the present and engage in rehearsals of future lives of their own creation.

We hope this book nurtures for our readers a space from which to explore, appreciate, and articulate ideas about young children's rights. This space may not always be a comfortable one, but true change requires embracing the unfamiliar. It is worth noting that this book developed as a dialogue between its two authors. During the course of more than 4 years, we talked about the content of this book over coffee. We shared our current experiences with the children in our lives, as well as our memories of the past and predictions for the future; fears as well as dreams, disappointments as well as visions. These exchanges pushed our thoughts beyond what would have been possible alone and resulted in new understandings for both of us. We hope that this book also inspires our readers to talk with others and reach a deeper and more thoughtful understanding of children's rights. To further this goal, each chapter ends with provocative discussion questions and activities that extend key ideas from the chapter.

We anticipate that the book will encourage critical thought, launch conversations, challenge behaviors that are not in line with beliefs, and remind us to question the necessity of social mores that fail to honor young children. When we remember to question the status quo, new ways of being and relating become possible.

CHAPTER 1

Tuning Adult Ears to the Voices of Young Children

FIGURE 1.1. A 4-year-old child demonstrating with his parents against the war in Iraq. © Boulder Journey School, 2010

At Boulder Journey School, efforts to understand how young children think about children's rights began in earnest in early 2003. Shortly after the United States began its military campaign in Iraq, a 4-year-old boy who demonstrated with his parents against the war carried a protest sign into his class at Boulder Journey School and declared, "1, 2, 3, 4 . . . we don't want your muddy war." The sign intrigued his classmates, one of whom asserted, "Soldiers don't have the right to kill other people." The teachers began to wonder what children thought about rights. They arranged an initial meeting of a small group of 4-year-olds and asked, "What is a right? If someone says, 'I have a right to do that,' or 'I have a right to think that way,' what does it mean?" (I. Hillman, 2003). The children discussed their ideas until they agreed on statements made by two children. One child stated, "A right is like you know in your heart it's okay to do it . . . you can do it if you want and that's it." Another child added, "But only if it's okay, like you won't hurt somebody and it's not safe . . . because the other person has a right to not be hurt too, right?" Over the ensuing weeks, the children compiled a list of their rights (Pufall, Rudkin, & Hall, 2004; Rudkin & Hall, 2005), which appears in Figure 1.2.

FIGURE 1.2. Boulder Journey School Charter on Children's Rights. © Boulder Journey School, 2010.

- Children have a right to plant flowers and plants with other people
- Children have a right to grow taller
- Children have a right to run or walk, to choose which one, if it's safe
- Children have a right to have friends
- Children have a right to touch everything, but gently, but not birds because that can scare them very much
- Children have a right to pretend that there's a beach anywhere
- Children have a right to pretend everything
- Children have a right to pretend with glass, but not a right to drop it 'cause that's not safe
- Children have a right to climb mountains, ski on the mountains (when there is snow), and play on the mountains (because the mountains are there for all of us to use)
- Children have a right to take off their clothes when they are hot, but not their socks
- Children have a right to have fun
- Children have a right to read books when they are crying (so they don't have to talk about it right away)
- Children have a right to sing, and to sing to other people
- Children have a right to help other people and even birds with broken wings (so it's okay for people to touch them)
- Children have a right to play all day
- Children have a right to twist their own ears, but not a right to twist other people's ears (a child must ask the other person first)
- Children have a right to be asked if someone wants to twist their ears
- Children have a right to guess how things work
- Children have a right to be in love and love each other

- Children have a right to eat grapes whichever way they choose, like peeling them first, if they want
- Children have a right to make ideas with other people
- Children have a right to be safe from fires and have firefighters ready to help them if there is a fire
- Children have a right to fall down when they feel like being crazy
- Children have a right to sleep when they are tired, or not to sleep when they are not tired, like just resting
- Children have a right to have their hair look like they want, but not a right to cut it unless they ask first
- Children have a right to choose their own clothes (and parents have a right to buy clothes for children if they want, but parents do not have a right to steal clothes)
- Children have a right to never, never go to jail
- Children have a right to pretend being dead and think about what it means to be dead
- Children have a right to eat some cheese or an apple when they are hungry
- Children have a right to good stuff that makes them happy
- Children have a right to clean air
- Children have a right to clean, fresh food to eat and if the food is dirty, they can say, 'NO!'
- Children have a right to clean, cold water or clean, hot water or clean, warm water
- Children have a right to chew soft gum, especially if it's the kind that cleans your teeth, but not a right to hard gum, like one might find at Copper Mountain's gumball machine
- Children have a right to talk, as long as they do not interrupt someone else who is talking first, but children have a right to wait for their turn to talk

FIGURE 1.2. Continued

- Children have a right to color with paint or markers and to choose which one
- Children have a right to eat brownies and make brownies
- Children have a right to get their own silverware
- Children have a right to brush their own teeth (and parents have a right to check their teeth when the children are done brushing)
- Children have a right to say, 'No!' or 'Stop it!' when people are tickling them without asking
- Children have a right to say, 'Yes!' when people tickle them, too
- Children have a right to have their words heard by other people
- Children have a right to be listened to
- Children have a right to walk away from people who are bothering them, but ask the bothering people to stop first to see if that works
- Children have a right to tell silly jokes
- Children have a right to build bridges out of peppers and other silly things with their lunch, if they can eat it, too
- Children have a right to know what time it is, and how many minutes they have to wait for something (their turn), and the time it will be when it's finally their turn

- Children have a right to wrestle or play fight, but not a right to punch (and maybe they can play rough on a bed)
- Children have a right to not be called names
- Children have a right to play tea parties, even with real tea
- Children have a right to crawl like kitties
- Children have a right to paint their fingernails, boys and girls, with their moms
- Children have a right to hug and kiss
- Children have a right to say, 'No' to mouth kisses
- Children have a right to play with Mom and Dad (after they are busy)
- Children have a right to watch kid TV shows, but not adult shows (because they are boring)
- Children have a right to watch adult TV shows if Mom or Dad say 'okay,' like Enterprise or Survivor
- Children have a right to watch movies, but not scary ones, but actually, they can watch a scary movie every once in a while
- Children have a right to tell parents and teachers to help them if they have a big problem
- Children have a right to solve their own problems whenever they can
- Children have a right to hang upside-down when it's safe

The sheer magnitude of the Boulder Journey School Charter on Children's Rights should dispel any notion of young children as empty vessels waiting to be filled with adult ideas, including ideas about their rights. The Charter on Children's Rights makes clear that young children have important insights into the issue of children's rights and how it pertains to their own lives. The profound thoughts of this small group of children led Boulder Journey School faculty to wonder, "How can we give voice to *all* the children at the school, including children who are preverbal?"

The Finnish educator Monika Riihela held that infants as young as 8 months have ideas to share. She asserted that every person, no matter how young, has stories to tell.

So it does not depend on the age of the teller, but on the sensitivity of the listener. A newborn baby is looking in your eyes, making silent questions, asking for cooperation for building a common world. That is the beginning of stories. (reported in Alderson, 2000b, pp. 26–27)

The literal meaning of "infant" is unable to speak, but children's "voices" can be heard from birth, provided adults take the time and effort to listen (Pugh & Selleck, 1996, p. 123). Researching the ideas of young children requires indirect methods of inquiry; one cannot simply ask children to talk about rights (Langsted, 1994; see also Clark & Moss, 2001). Nevertheless, children of all ages offer valuable insights about rights, if society can become attuned to children's ways of communicating (McLeod, 2008).

LISTENING TO YOUNG CHILDREN

A children's rights movement must be as much about "adult ears" as it is about "children's voices" (R. Hart, 1998, cited in Miljeteig, 2000, p. 171). At Boulder Journey School, our research on children's rights has led us to specify four suggestions for tuning adult ears to the voices of young children.

Listening Creatively: Can Adults Appreciate Children's Many Languages?

Adult society relies on the spoken and written word. Parents note and celebrate a child's first words, but rarely mark other hallmarks in communication, such as the first time a child points to request an object or represents something by imitating it, for example, flapping her or his arms to signify a bird (Doherty-Sneddon, 2003). Listening to young children means appreciating that they communicate using a wide array of languages. If children do indeed speak using 100 languages, then in order to understand what children are saying, adults must listen with all of *their* creativity. Rinaldi (2001) proposed "listening not just with our ears but with all our senses (sight, touch, smell, taste, orientation). Listening to the hundred, the thousand languages" (p. 80).

In working to appreciate the perspectives of young children, verbal language proves to be a source of misunderstanding, as well as understanding. As an example of misunderstanding, one teacher seeking insight into the perspectives of 2- and 3-year-old children began a conversation on rights using a book about a mouse named Toby. For each page of the book, she mapped Toby's experience onto the issue of rights. For example, on the page depicting Toby and his mother embracing, the teacher said, "Toby has the right to hug his mother." At the end of the book, she invited the children to consider their rights. One girl responded by drawing lines on the book with her finger and calling out the names of letters. It took the teacher a few minutes to realize the child had confused the word "rights" with the more familiar word "writes."

As a second example of misunderstanding, several teachers decided to avoid the use of the word "rights" in their research with 3- and 4-year-old children. They asked instead, "Is it okay to be happy? . . . Is it okay to be sad? . . . Is it okay to be angry?" The teachers had seen evidence of the children asserting their right to anger and sadness and so were surprised by the children's insistence that it was okay to be happy but *not* okay to be sad or to be angry. The question, "Is it okay to be?" has very different connotations, however, than the question, "Do you have a right to be?" Children's assertions that sadness and anger were not okay may stem from their awareness that these emotions were not always okay with their parents or teachers or peers, or that being angry or sad did not feel okay to them. The children nevertheless might have believed that they had a *right* to be angry and sad as well as happy.

Children's unfamiliarity with abstract terms and their more concrete use of language can impede child–adult understanding. On the other hand, children's use of language can elucidate the issues at hand with a poet's precision. Consider the following exchange among three 5-year-olds:

> *First Child:* I would like to have a car that is my size with really big wheels. I can drive my daddy to school and then I can go to McDonald's and eat french fries.
> *Second Child:* Wow! . . . I would like to have a room that is my size. I would like it if I could climb in my bed without my daddy picking me up . . .
> *Third Child:* . . . I would like a sink on the floor.

These children were speaking about the dependence on adults that arises, not from lack of competence, but from their small stature in an adult-sized world. The third child seemed to be requesting, in a poetic way, not an actual sink on the floor but autonomy in performing the daily task of hand washing. This dialogue illustrates that "'listening' to very young children does not necessarily mean taking all their utterances at face value, but it does mean observing the nuances" (Pugh & Selleck, 1996, p. 121).

Boulder Journey School educators provide numerous materials to facilitate children's communication in a variety of languages, including drawing, painting, clay work, wire sculpting, photography, and manipulations of natural materials and blocks. Examples appear throughout this book, but let us include one drawing here.

A classroom of 2-year-olds at Boulder Journey School received a gift from a family member, and the teacher helped the children write a letter of appreciation. They then took a class trip to mail their letter. When the children arrived at the mailbox, they were dismayed to find that it loomed far out of their reach. The children did not want the teacher to lift them up to reach it, resulting in a long-term investigation exploring how children could mail a letter independently. Ultimately, they agreed on the use of a stepstool. During this investigation, one of the children

FIGURE 1.3. A 2-year-old child's drawing of a mailbox towering high atop a very long post. © Boulder Journey School, 2010.

drew a picture (Figure 1.3) depicting with poignant precision a mailbox towering high atop a very long post. Like the poetic notion of a sink on the floor, this drawing conveys with artistic precision the sense of smallness that children often experience in the world of adults.

In addition to providing children with opportunities to use a multitude of languages, educators have gained insights into young children's understanding of rights through careful "listening" to children's behavior. A teacher of 1-year-olds, for example, watched her students play in the school theater where hobbyhorses are stored in tall buckets beyond the children's reach. Children of many ages, including the 1-year-olds, enjoy using these hobbyhorses to pretend and play. The teacher noticed that the children persisted in trying to obtain these objects by hovering nearby, pointing, tugging at the parts of the toy they could reach, and vocalizing. She hypothesized that the children believed they had a right to use the horses, and contrasted their persistence in trying to obtain the horses with their lack of persistence in obtaining desired objects to which the children did not feel entitled, such as classmates' bottles.

In listening to children's behavior, adults must attend closely to their play. Developmental psychologists and early childhood educators increasingly understand that play is crucial to the well-being and development of children, and is the main activity through which children seek and find meaning (E. Jones & Reynolds, 1992; Wenner, 2009). The play theorist Brian Sutton-Smith wrote that because "children up until about seven years of age communicate with each other more adequately by play than in speech, an argument can certainly be made that their childhood right to play is the same as our adult First Amendment right to free speech" (quoted in Nabhan & Trimble, 1994, p. 9).

Authors of the Charter on Children's Rights also recognized the importance of play in children's lives. They declared, "Children have a right to pretend everything," and "Children have a right to play all day."

Listening Patiently: Can Adults Appreciate the Significance of Time?

Children's rights researcher Priscilla Alderson (2000a) listed numerous barriers to children's rights, including language barriers and adults' fear of losing control. A perceived lack of time was, however, first on the list. At Boulder Journey School, teachers repeatedly report that a commitment to honoring children's rights means appreciating the importance of slowing down. Here is one example.

A teacher of 1-year-olds decided to analyze archival photos of her classroom as a means of listening to what infants were saying about their rights. The teacher noticed that although the infants had all become mobile, photographs still depicted adults carrying infants from place to place. She wondered if the teachers' well-intentioned inclination to carry children illustrated a lack of respect for the children's right to autonomy. For the next scheduled trip to the theater, teachers in this classroom offered children the opportunity to travel on their own, either by crawling or walking along the low ballet bars in the hallway. In order to maximize the chances of children completing their journey, teachers departed 30 minutes before their scheduled visit to the theater. They found that it actually took less time for the children to arrive at the theater under their own power than it had for the teachers to carry them two by two. Which is not to advocate 1-year-olds transporting themselves on the grounds of efficiency. In this case, children arrived at the theater quickly, but letting children exercise autonomy often requires patience.

Listening to and respecting the rights of children means providing time. It may take time for children to exercise autonomy when they are mastering such new skills as crawling or walking down hallways, climbing into car seats, putting on socks and shoes, or washing their hands. Similarly, it may take time for children to express their thoughts and desires, especially when using a language that is not yet well developed. It also takes time for adults to understand the languages that children may prefer, such as creative expression and play. Adults may have neglected and forgotten these languages in the course of growing up.

Listening in the Here and Now: Can Adults Attend to Context?

Patience not only opens opportunities for children to exercise their competencies, it also demonstrates a respect for children's agendas. Adults and children live with different orientations to time. Adult society is future-oriented. Adults tend to concern themselves with upcoming appointments, undone tasks, and even more distant events such as their children's enrollment in college and their own retirement. Children, on the other hand, are sensitive to the wonders of the here and now, wonders for which they eagerly forego other agendas (e.g., Langsted, 1994). They exist in the moment and focus on what they find before them. Children encounter numerous marvels on the way to the car or to the store that merit examination—the intriguing shapes and splashes of puddles, the intricate pathways of bugs and worms, the irresistible gleams of shining treasures lying on the street disguised as trash.

Differing orientations to time can create challenges for adults and children alike. The adults' desire to hurry easily eclipses the child's momentary fascinations, and it can be difficult for adults to share authentically the focus of children's interests. The challenge of integrating different time orientations led one adult writer to describe childhood as a time when "the days are endless and the years fly by" (Schiff, 2003).

As an example of children's fascination with what lies immediately before them, consider the experiences of a Boulder Journey School teacher interested in helping 2-year-olds express themselves through the language of photography. The mechanics of taking a photograph challenge young children, who may find the size and heft of the camera awkward and the closing of one eye in order to look

FIGURE 1.4. Photography may be challenging for young children. © Boulder Journey School, 2010.

through the viewfinder difficult. This teacher found that as the children manipulated the camera, their fingers often got in the way of the lens. On one occasion a child's finger obscured the lens almost entirely. As the teacher and child reviewed this photograph, the teacher began to advise the child on how to hold the camera more effectively, while the child erupted in elation over the results. "It's my finger!" he exclaimed. His classmates shared his excitement. "Take a picture of my finger next."

Given children's attentiveness to the here and now, educators at Boulder Journey School have found that children's discussions, including discussions of rights, are particularly rich when they center on issues salient for children at that moment. This often can be attributed to their development (e.g., issues of mobility or sharing) or based on current events in the school or in the home (e.g., a new class pet or the birth of a sibling). Similarly, specific questions are best explored when the children are in a context relevant to the questions at hand: talking about the class pet while in front of its cage, for example, or considering the ethics of sharing while arguments over a toy are fresh in the children's minds (see Langsted, 1994).

During lunch, one teacher invited 4-year-old children to consider children's rights around mealtime decisions. Mealtime certainly constitutes an important area of inquiry, as numerous entries in the Boulder Journey School Charter on Children's Rights concern food. The teacher asked, "How would having a say in

FIGURE 1.5. Teachers invited 3-year-old children into the infant classroom to play, observe, and reflect on infants' rights. © Boulder Journey School, 2010.

what food is packed in your lunch make you feel and why?" Most children did not currently have input into the content of their lunches, but wanted input, and gave answers that suggested they would make responsible choices. One girl who said she would choose to pack fruit noted, "Big apples make you bigger because they are healthy."

The teacher also asked, "Would you enjoy deciding when you eat your lunch at school and why?" He had reasoned that the requirement that children eat together at an adult-determined time was not respectful of the children's autonomy. The teacher hypothesized that children would welcome the chance to decide on mealtimes for themselves. The children's responses surprised him. Children thought it more important to share mealtime with friends than to eat when they were hungry. As one boy responded, "I love Nicholas and Natalie. It is important to eat with friends and it's sad without."

Another example of the importance of immediate context emerged in a project seeking insight into preverbal infants' perspectives through the eyes of older children. Teachers brought two 3-year-old children into the infant classroom to play, observe, and reflect on infants' rights. The teachers initiated the conversation by asking the older children what infants could do. When they were interviewed in the infant classroom, the older children generated 25 ideas about what infants could do. They noted, for example, that infants could "shake and clap when they are happy," and "play together and by themselves." The older children had very few ideas about infants' competencies, however, when interviewed in a quiet conference room away from the infants.

FIGURE 1.6. Children are inherently social at the earliest of ages. ©
Boulder Journey School, 2010.

Listening to Collective (as Well as Individual) Voices: Can Adults Honor Children's Social Lives?

Traditional notions of psychosocial development conceptualize children as essentially presocial (i.e., egocentric and in need of training in empathy and perspective-taking) or as antisocial (i.e., egocentric and in need of adult-imposed social mores) (Oakley, 1994). At Boulder Journey School, however, we find children to be inherently social at the earliest of ages and, beginning in infancy, children spend much of their school day working together in pairs and small groups.

From the initial exchanges among children discussing the antiwar sign to the conversations in the subsequent projects described throughout this book, insights into the perspectives of children were gleaned primarily from one or more teachers interacting with children in small groups. Children continually asserted, counter-asserted, built on one another's ideas, and revised their thinking. In small-group gatherings, children showed their caring for one another and their ability to listen to and support one another's conceptualizations (see also Mayall, 2000a). As the authors of the Boulder Journey School Charter on Children's Rights observed, "Children have a right to make ideas with other people."

Lev Vygotsky (1978) enriched developmental psychology immeasurably by conceptualizing learning as a social transaction. Key to his theory is the notion of the *zone of proximal development* (ZPD), defined as "the distance between the actual development level as determined by independent problem solving and the level of potential development as determined through problem solving under adult guidance or in collaboration with more capable peers" (p. 86). Although educators at Boulder Journey School find the notion of ZPD useful, we have questioned two tenets. First, we wonder why only *independent* problem solving indicates "actual developmental level" (why not joint problem solving?). Second, we find that enhanced competence does not require "more capable peers"—only *companionable* peers. In our work with children at Boulder Journey School we find that when working together, peers at similar levels of development build ideas and enhance one another's understanding of the world around them.

The notion that children build ideas and gain insight through discussion with peers, although consistent with the social constructivist perspective of Boulder Journey School, runs counter to traditional views of children as antisocial or presocial. It also runs counter to the preferred methodologies of traditional research: large-scale assessments of isolated individuals who either fill out a questionnaire alone at a desk or participate in a one-on-one interview with the researcher in a quiet and secluded room. Such methodologies remove children from relevant contexts and prevent them from exhibiting their collective competence. The preference for such isolating assessment techniques may help explain why "tests of children show far fewer capabilities than children exhibit in the course of the day, in conversation" (Alderson, 2000b, p. 82).

CHILDREN'S INSIGHTS ABOUT CHILDREN'S RIGHTS

It is all too easy to miss the voices of children, and the four suggestions for listening delineated above do not constitute an exhaustive list. One also might make a case for the importance of attentiveness, openness, flexibility, and numerous other qualities. Perhaps the core component of true listening is a willingness to learn from and be changed by what the other says. When adults position ourselves far above the children in our lives, we risk creating chasms too wide for young children to breech. When adults assume attitudes that are in any way dismissive, judgmental, or all-knowing, we may silence all but the most outspoken of children and risk that even those brave voices fall on deaf ears.

The authors believe that young children are far more competent than most adults imagine. We hope to show throughout this book that young children understand, and have much to teach adults, about the notion of rights. In this first chapter we have seen that children recognize the importance of their right to self-expression. Authors of the Boulder Journey School Charter on Children's Rights asserted, "Children have a right to have their words heard by other people," and "Children have a right to be listened to." The authors also recognize that children speak in nonverbal as well as verbal languages, declaring, "Children have a right to color with paint or markers and to choose which one," and "Children have a right to sing, and to sing to other people." Furthermore, children understand that rights, including the right to self-expression, are not contingent on age. As noted earlier, several 2- and 3-year-olds observed that even infants express themselves, conveying their emotions and ideas by shaking and clapping.

Young children not only appreciate the importance of self-expression, they also demonstrate a keen awareness of the delicate balances required by the notion of rights. One tension we explore throughout this book is the need to balance children's perspectives and adults' perspectives. Children demonstrate an astute awareness of the privileges and responsibilities of the adults in their lives. In the Charter on Children's Rights, for example, children stated, "Children have a right to brush their own teeth (and parents have a right to check their teeth when the children are done brushing)." As another example, for the project in which 2- and 3-year-olds reflected on the rights of infants, the teachers offered the older children markers and paper and encouraged storytelling and drawing. The following story resulted.

> Maggie was looking at a beautiful butterfly and she wanted to touch it, but she couldn't walk. What if Walter saw a friendly spider but he couldn't get it because he didn't know how to walk? They couldn't walk and the teacher had to come and get them closer.

These young children expressed the sophisticated notion (explored further in the section in Chapter 2 on disability rights) that infants have a right to experience their environments despite their lack of mobility, and that adults have a responsibility to foster infants' participation in the world around them.

A second tension inherent to children's rights is the need to balance protection rights and participation rights (a focus of Chapter 3). Young children understand this balance as well. They believe that they should be able to make choices, but that these choices are constrained by concerns for safety. For example, one right listed in the Boulder Journey School Charter on Children's Rights is, "Children have a right to pretend with glass, but not a right to drop it 'cause that's not safe." And another: "Children have a right to run or walk, to choose which one, if it's safe." Children also understand that the manifestation of rights, particularly protection rights, changes across development. Older children appreciated the greater need for protection earlier in life. As one 3-year-old working with the infants noted, "We have to keep babies from choking."

A third tension that recurs throughout this book is the tension between individual liberties and communal responsibilities (see Chapter 4). Children are eager to live and work with others, especially other children, and show a keen sensitivity to varying perspectives. As one of many examples of children's ability to hold different viewpoints in balance, consider this entry in the Charter on Children's Rights: "Children have a right to talk, as long as they do not interrupt someone else who is talking first, but children have a right to wait for their turn to talk." Each of these tensions is explored in the theoretical discussion of the first four chapters, and illustrated in the two more applied chapters that follow.

CONCLUSION

The work on children's rights that children and educators at Boulder Journey School began in earnest in 2003 continues to this day, and the Boulder Journey

School Charter on Children's Rights remains central to our work. The authors have shared this Charter, and the projects that followed, with students, teachers, conference participants, other children, family members, and now with you, the reader of this book. The Charter hangs prominently in the hallway of Boulder Journey School, conveying children's ideas about their rights to all who pass by, and it has served as a daily reminder to the authors of what we are writing about and why.

For Further Thought

1. Think of a time when, as a child, you didn't think your rights were supported. Describe the event and how it made you feel.
2. Recall an instance when you witnessed a child's rights being disregarded. Describe the occurrence, how you felt, and what you did or could have done to support the child.
3. Think of an occasion when you were surprised by a child's competence. Discuss the occasion and what it means in terms of your assumptions about children and/or your images of children. In this instance, what do you think enabled you to tune your ears to children's voices?
4. Which entry in the Boulder Journey School Charter on Children's Rights stands out most for you? Why do you think this entry is notable? Share the Boulder Journey School Charter on Children's Rights with a child or group of children and ask the same question.

CHAPTER 2

Children's Rights in the United States: Learning from the Social Movements of the 1960s

Several years ago, while I was hiking in the mountains of Colorado and humming "This Little Light of Mine" to myself, my thinking about children's rights shifted. I was struck by the many ways that the struggle for children's rights parallels the struggles of other marginalized groups in the United States. A consideration of children's rights in the context of other rights movements has led to innumerable conversations with friends, relatives, and acquaintances. Sometimes the conversations are short, ending with my conversation partner's raised eyebrows and admission, "That's interesting." Other times I feel misunderstood, as my conversation partner ties the notion of children's oppression to heartbreaking images of children in other lands, laboring endless hours to weave rugs or carrying weapons into the trenches of wars that long precede their birth. This is not the terrain of children's rights that the authors of this book traverse each day or the terrain we feel most competent to navigate through conversation and writing. We believe that a lack of respect for children's rights compromises the lives of all children everywhere. Our goal in writing this book is to understand more completely the implications of children's rights for the children in our own lives . . . and maybe in yours. Our hope is that readers will make connections to their own experiences with children in contexts beyond the context of this book's authors.

CHILDREN'S RIGHTS AND NEW CONVERSATIONS: IN PRAISE OF STUTTERING

It is important to note that despite a view of children's rights violations as occurring in distant lands, the United States remains one of only two countries worldwide (the other country is Somalia) that have failed to ratify the landmark 1989 United Nations Convention on the Rights of the Child (UNCRC).[1] Indeed, the authors have found that many people with whom we talk—learned people in the fields of child development and education—have never heard of the UNCRC. This seems remarkable in a country that considers itself the leader of world democracy.

Not only has the United States failed to ratify the landmark UNCRC, it does not yet have any national policy concerning the rights of children (Walker, Brooks, & Wrightsman, 1999). Contrast this situation with, for example, the children's rights policies of Denmark. The Danish Ministry of Social Affairs, which oversees all early childhood services in that nation, distributes to all children under its jurisdiction a series of pamphlets based on the UNCRC. An excerpt from the pamphlet for children aged 3 to 6 reads:

> Grown-ups have lots of set ideas about how things should be organized. But children have their own ideas, and grown-ups must listen to children's ideas. Grown-ups must listen to what children have to say. Children must also have a say in things. (cited in Langsted, 1994, p. 30)

The children's rights movement in the United States has focused on protection and provision rights: Children have the right to be protected from maltreatment, for example, and to be provided with food and shelter. These rights are consistent with struggles for *human* rights. *Civil* rights, on the other hand, center on participation. Participation rights, unlike protection and provision rights, involve visibility and voice, having a say about what happens to oneself and one's communities. Participation rights in many ways are opposed to protection rights—the latter seeking to shield and insulate, the former to involve and include (the tension between protection and participation is examined further in the next chapter).

The UNCRC recognizes the need to protect children from abuse, neglect, and exploitation, and to provide children with basic security and life opportunities. But the UNCRC also enumerates far-reaching participation rights. Article 12 asserts:

> States Parties shall assure to the child who is capable of forming his or her own views the right to express those views freely in all matters affecting the child, the views of the child being given due weight in accordance with the age and maturity of the child. (Office of the United Nations High Commission for Human Rights, 1989)

The UNCRC claims for children the freedom of expression and also other freedoms, such as freedom to access information, freedom of thought, freedom of religion, and freedom of association. Such lofty and abstract notions of freedom suggest public stages and policy debates, but that is not the main arena for the implementation of human rights. Eleanor Roosevelt (1953) asked:

> Where after all do human rights begin? In small places, close to home—so small that they cannot be seen on any map of the world. Yet they are the world of the individual person. . . . Unless these rights have meaning there, they have little meaning anywhere.

The authors believe that it is in everyday exchanges with children that a commitment to children's rights rings true or hollow. These everyday exchanges are not usually uplifting heart-to-heart discussions or endearing moments of bonding. The exchanges that require an irreversible shift in perspective are more often irritating or uncomfortable. Like the afternoon I returned home late and told my 2-year-old son, "Okay, you have a choice. Would you like to take a bath now or eat dinner?" He looked at me calmly and responded, "There are more choices than that."

The children's rights lawyer Jeremy Roche (1996) warned, "Critically, once we genuinely allow children to exercise their right to speak and be heard, we might have to participate in new conversations" (p. 33). New conversations can be disorienting. They may come during the rushed starts of busy mornings, or at the dizzying ends of tiring days. Or, at some point in between where they threaten to interrupt the relentless rhythm of what the philosopher Al Gini (2003) called our "everydayathon." Such interruptions are more easily quashed and forgotten than honored.

New conversations demand time, space, and energy. They call on us to surrender our assumptive worlds, to question what moments before seemed to be a given, to accommodate disturbance. That is why new conversations are the cornerstone of social change. "It is a matter of introducing a kind of awkwardness into the fabric of one's experience, of interrupting the fluency of the narratives that encode that experience and making them stutter" (Nikolas Rose, cited in Moss & Petrie, 2002, p. 11).

To be questioned, disturbed, challenged, and at a loss for words can leave a person feeling wrong, perhaps foolish. This feeling may be hardest to accommodate when interacting with children. In front of children, adults expect to appear as knowing and in control. Adult social power allows parents, teachers, and others to unthinkingly quell the legitimate uprisings of children. The authors of this book have come to believe that social power accruing from membership in the social group "adult" is not entirely different from social power afforded to people who are White, or male, or able-bodied. It therefore would follow that a movement for children's rights could benefit from a consideration of other social movements, such as the Black civil rights movement, the women's movement, and the disability rights movement.

Interestingly, the treatment of children serves as a gauge by which we measure the ill treatment of other disenfranchised groups. The closer a group's treatment approximates our treatment of children, the greater its oppression. The word "boy" assumes a knifelike edge when used to refer to a Black man. The word "girl" feels disrespectful and demeaning when used to refer to a woman. People with disabilities may exclaim in anguish, "Stop treating me like a child!" If by saying, "Don't treat me like a child," protesters mean to say, "Don't treat me as less than you, as incompetent and inferior," the authors argue that we should stop treating children like children.

We do not claim that the oppression of children is the *same* as the oppression of other groups. We do think, however, that when we consider the possibility of a link among various oppressions, some surprising similarities emerge alongside the differences.

DYNAMICS OF OPPRESSION:
"OUR SIMILARITIES ARE DIFFERENT"

Several classic texts published in the 1960s and early 1970s argued that systems of oppression create prescribed ways for people in more powerful social positions and people in less powerful social positions to relate to each other. Albert Memmi (1965/1967) explored patterns of domination through the lens of colonization. William Ryan (1971) described the phenomenon of victim-blaming as social circumstances that are attributed to the personal deficits of people in oppressed groups. Paulo Freire (1970/1992) showed how people in less powerful social groups could interrupt the dynamics of oppression through dialogue and education. All of this groundbreaking work has led to the identification of numerous common elements of oppression, such as a defined norm against which members of oppressed groups are compared and found to fall short; the use of violence and the threat of violence to keep oppressed groups in their place; and the oppressed group's internalization of negative images and stereotypes (e.g., Pharr, 1988).

Although many dynamics of oppression transcend membership in a particular group, the specifics of how the dynamic plays out have a distinct character. The psychologist James Jones (1994) began a chapter on appreciating diversity with a quote from Yogi Berra's son: "I am a lot like him, only our similarities are different" (p. 27). When it comes to social groups struggling for human and civil rights, the similarities are indeed different.

Consider, for example, invisibility and voicelessness. Although all oppressed groups experience invisibility and voicelessness, each group experiences it in a unique way. Ralph Ellison's (1947) novel *Invisible Man* described how prejudice prevented White people from acknowledging the humanity of the Black narrator, who lived a shadow life. He began his story:

> I am an invisible man. . . . I am a man of substance, of flesh and bone, fiber and liquids—and I might even be said to possess a mind. I am invisible, understand, simply because people refuse to see me. (p. 3)

Invisibility is a key issue in the lives of people with disabilities as well. In a chapter entitled "A Hidden Army for Civil Rights," Joseph Shapiro (1993) contended that the refusal to see those among us with physical disabilities is reinforced by environmental barriers. People with physical disabilities are excluded from participation in society by curbs, stairs, and, in the extreme, institutionalization (see Johnson, 2003). This is the same as, and also different from, the way women have been kept voiceless and unseen. Women are denied full participation when their rightful place is deemed to be in the home, preferably, as the adage goes, "barefoot and pregnant."

Young people, too, are often invisible and voiceless. Exclusion is both institutional and interpersonal. Young people are not represented in most governments. Few outlets exist for children's meaningful involvement in community life. And the possibilities for inclusion, even in day-to-day social transactions, are limited further for very young children. Parents spend several years lifting small children over too-high countertops in banks, post offices, cafeterias, and even ice cream parlors. Adults ask, "How old is he?" long after children reach an age where they can answer such questions for themselves. And one may hear grown-ups announce to one another, "Isn't she cute!" as if the child before them were unable to hear the conversation in the space above her head. Most have heard the old adage, "Children should be seen and not heard." In his book *Unconditional Parenting*, Alfie Kohn (2005) recalled overhearing a plane passenger commending a parent upon landing for having a child who was so *good* during the flight. Kohn observed that the word "good" is imbued with moral significance and can mean ethical, honorable, or compassionate. "However, where children are concerned, the word is just as likely to mean nothing more than *quiet*—or perhaps, *not a pain in the butt to me*" (p. 2). In the Boulder Journey School Charter on Children's Rights (see Chapter 1), children resisted their imposed silence, stating "Children have a right to have their words heard by other people," and "Children have a right to be listened to."

Linking the oppression of different groups is a risky enterprise. To some it seems to diminish the importance of a particular group's experience. The authors hope that our exploration of children's rights in the context of other rights movements does not minimize the hardship any other group has undergone or dilute the heroism of that group's freedom fighters. Indeed, we believe it is even *more* imperative for those of us interested in commonalities in the dynamics of oppression to recognize and respect each group's separateness, each group's own history, resources, challenges, and relationship to the larger society. We also believe, however, that considering possible commonalities in the dynamics of oppression leads us to appreciate instructive points of intersection. The remainder of this chapter examines lessons for the children's rights movement from three other movements: the Black civil rights movement, the women's movement, and the disability rights movement.

Learning from the Black Civil Rights Movement: "This Little Light of Mine"

The activist and scholar Vincent Harding (1990) described the Black civil rights movement as a gift to all groups fighting oppression. Lessons learned from the civil rights movement have informed every subsequent movement for social change (Adams, Bell, & Griffin, 1997). Since the 1950s, the Black civil rights movement has served as a model for the civil rights struggles of women, American Indians, Chicanos, lesbian and gay people, people with disabilities, poor people, and antiwar activists. The Black civil rights movement also has influenced the struggle against age-based discrimination, but primarily for those on the older side of the age continuum. For example, in choosing the name "Gray Panthers," senior citizen activists paid homage to the Black Panthers.

The struggle for children's rights, however, has not often been tied to the Black civil rights movement. This is in some ways surprising. Young people are often the vanguard of struggles for freedom (e.g., Harding, 1990; Rudkin, 2003), but youthful warriors usually stand at the threshold of adulthood—people in their late teens or 20s. In the Black civil rights movement, young children counted among the most prominent freedom fighters. The plaintiff in the Supreme Court's landmark 1954 *Brown v. Board of Education* decision was Linda Brown, a child seeking the right to attend her local elementary school. Norman Rockwell popularized the image of 7-year-old Ruby Bridges in her starched white dress, flanked by armed federal marshals, walking a daily gauntlet of cursing White people on her way to integrate a New Orleans school. In the spring of 1963, so many young people participated in the civil rights marches of Birmingham, Alabama, that the struggle became known as The Children's Crusade (see Mayer, 2008). Nine-year old Audrey Faye Hendricks, one among thousands of child protesters, was perhaps the youngest crusader arrested. She spent 7 days in jail (Levine, 1993).

To some degree, Black children *participated* in the civil rights movement because *protection* was not an option. While White children could remain distant from the civil rights battles raging around them, as they could remain protected from the ravages of racism, the impact on Black children was direct and immediate. Ruby Bridges (1999) opened her autobiography with the line, "When I was six years old, the civil rights movement came knocking at the door" (p. 4). Similarly, Audrey Faye Hendricks recalled, "There was no way for me not to know about the movement." Her mother served as secretary of their church, which was active in the civil rights movement. "When there was news of bombs, we would all go, my mother, my father, my little baby sister, and me. No matter what time of night, we were always part of it" (Levine, 1993, p. 78).

Although the relevance of the Black civil rights movement to children's rights remains unexamined, the authors believe that numerous lessons can be gleaned. This section touches on four: the need to reject negative images and stereotypes, the importance of creative expression, the power of recognizing gaps between rhetoric and action, and the crucial roles members of the oppressed group can play in uncovering injustice (there are, of course, many other lessons, such as the power of nonviolent protest, the importance of grassroots organizing, and the possibility of advancing equality through the legal system).

For all their differences, two of the Black civil rights movement's most visible leaders, Martin Luther King, Jr., and Malcolm X, both believed that the condition of African American people in the United States would change only after overcoming internalized oppression (Cone, 1991). Before demanding equal rights, members of marginalized groups first must believe themselves worthy of respect and fair treatment. The need to replace internalized oppression and private suffering with self-respect and collective action is one lesson from the Black civil rights movement with profound implications for the movement for children's rights.

The Reggio Emilia approach to education that inspires Boulder Journey School carefully considers the "image of the child." Educators repeatedly find that when adults think of (and treat) children as capable, resourceful, and powerful, rather than immature, egocentric, and in need of adult control, children show themselves to be exquisitely competent. This is consistent with a wealth of recent research into children's capabilities. As researchers develop better assessment techniques, children prove to be more competent at younger ages than previously thought (e.g., Alderson, 2000b; Kagan, 1994).

As described in Chapter 1, honoring the competence of children requires careful listening to many modes of expression. Children express themselves in a wondrous array of languages, including poetry, painting, movement, and music. Other marginalized groups also rely on creative expression. In the Black civil rights movement, music was perhaps the most influential "language" of liberation. Freedom songs, many of which derived from spirituals sung by Black people during slavery, energized that movement and continue to be sung when members of oppressed groups come together to confront social injustice. Spirituals, and the protest songs they inspired, convey revolutionary messages. Consider, for example, "All God's Children Got Shoes," also called "Heaven, Heaven"— a song that, like many other freedom songs, has become popular as a *children's* song (and isn't that interesting?).

> I got shoes
> You got shoes
> All God's children got shoes
> When I get to heaven gonna put on my shoes
> Gonna walk all over God's Heaven, Heaven, Heaven!
> Everybody talkin' 'bout Heaven ain't going there,
> Heaven, Heaven
> Gonna walk all over God's Heaven!

The simple lyrics cloak bold challenges to slavery and oppression. Slaves did not have many belongings, often going without shoes, let alone such luxuries as the robes, harps, and crowns God's children display in subsequent verses of the song. The lyrics conjure a new world where people who currently have very little partake in abundance, and those who currently enjoy wealth are called to task. The basis for this reversal is revealed in the line, "Everybody talkin' 'bout heaven ain't goin' there." This line directly challenges the hypocrisy of slaveholders who gathered together in holy worship to celebrate God on Sunday mornings, and returned to the plantation in the afternoon where they engaged in the immoral and inhumane treatment of their fellow human beings. The song implies that there will be no place in the new and just world for people who subscribe to Godly rhetoric but perpetuate an un-Godly reality. In a new, just world the tables will turn and slaveholders will be the ones going without while the liberated children of God walk in shoes, wear robes, don wings, and rejoice (A. Jones, 1993).

On that fateful mountain hike that changed my thinking about children and their rights (recounted in the opening of this chapter), I found myself humming the spiritual, "This Little Light of Mine." I remembered an interview between the television personality Bill Moyers and Bernice Johnson Reagon, an activist, freedom singer, scholar, and founder of the a cappella group Sweet Honey in the Rock.

Moyers characterized "This Little Light of Mine" as a song of humility—my light may not be very big, but I can let it do the small work it can. Reagon greeted this misinterpretation with hearty laughter. She stated that in a world where Black people are supposed to be invisible, the statement, "'This little light of mine, I'm gonna let it shine' is just crashing through all of that. It is a very arrogant stance. Everywhere I go I'm gonna let it shine" (Reagon, 1991). "This Little Light of Mine" reminds me of the importance of confronting efforts to silence children with adult power, efforts that, embarrassingly enough, I sometimes confront in myself.

When my older son was almost 4, he moved to a new classroom where he was the youngest instead of the oldest. Within a few days a new word took over his vocabulary: "poop." The sudden prevalence of this word was surprising. There was no telling what would trigger it. "Are your shoes feeling tight?" I might ask, never expecting the response of, "Poop, poop, POOP." Occasionally, this was the sole word in lengthy and animated monologues that got intermittently louder, as if his younger brother were fiddling with his volume dial: Poop, poop, poop, poop, Poop, POOP, poop, poop, POOOOP!!

My partner and I tried ignoring it. We tried discussing it. We tried cordoning off times when it was okay to use the word (in the bathroom or when talking with friends who also liked the word) and times when it was *not* okay (at dinner). We tried using it as an opportunity to practice writing (write it, don't say it). Nothing seemed to help.

I tried to see the situation from my son's perspective and determined to react calmly, but my patience sometimes wore thin. One afternoon, I had had enough. "Stop," I exclaimed. "You know I don't want to hear that word. Save that talk for your little friends." To my surprise, he did stop. Then he asked me a question: "Why did you call my friends 'little'?" They *are* of relatively small stature, but that's not what I meant, and he knew it. Just two letters separate "little" from "belittle." My son confirmed that the word made him feel bad, and I promised not to call his friends "little" again.

Paulo Freire (1970/1992) noted that people with social power rarely relinquish power on their own. Indeed, they/we may not even notice the power that they/we wield. Vincent Harding (1990) argued that the Black civil rights movement presented an opportunity for White citizens to confront the oppressive power they held, however unwittingly, and thereby save their souls. According to Harding, the movement was, above all else, an effort to reveal the gap between the rhetoric and reality of the United States, an unwavering call for Americans to walk their talk. This, Harding asserted, was the movement's greatest gift. And, it is a gift that each of us can pass on, one person to another. Harding (1990) reflected,

> There are times in our experience when we are living lives which contradict and deny the best truths that we claim for ourselves. Therefore we are crippling ourselves, damaging our spirits, but have grown accustomed to the process. At such times, people in our families, or those unfamiliar to us, may offer a magnificent opportunity for us to disturb and re-collect ourselves and return to our most authentic commitments, when they challenge our direction, when they

refuse to cooperate with our self-destructive actions, or our equally damaging acts against them. (p. 111)

Children frequently, although often quietly, offer adults such gifts. They offer us such precious and uncomfortable opportunities to redeem ourselves, if only we can find the grace to listen.

Learning from the Second Women's Movement: "The Personal Is Political"

Just as the dynamics of oppression take on a distinct character in relation to each oppressed group, so too must different civil rights battles cover different terrain. Thus, proponents of children's rights can learn not only from the Black civil rights movement, but from other movements as well.

Numerous parallels exist between struggles for Black rights and women's rights, including intersections in the timelines of these struggles. In the first half of the 19th century, the women's suffrage and antislavery movements co-occurred. Several activists, notably the ex-slaves Frederick Douglass and Sojourner Truth, participated in both. More than 100 years later, when social upheaval was in the air and the Black civil rights movement offered a powerful model for protest, the second-wave women's movement also gained momentum.

Like activists in the Black civil rights movement of the 1950s and 1960s, spokespeople from both the abolitionist and suffrage movements of the previous century propelled their causes by appealing to the gap between rhetoric and reality. Notably, activists of the era pointed out the hypocrisy of denying rights to Black people and women in a country founded on proclamations of equality evident in the Declaration of Independence. In a speech given on July 4, 1829, the 53rd anniversary of the signing of the Declaration of Independence, the abolitionist William Lloyd Garrison declared, "Sirs, I am not come to tell you that slavery is a curse, debasing in its effect, cruel in its operation, fatal in its continuance. The day and the occasion require no such revelation. I do not claim the discovery as my own, that 'all men are born equal'" (pp. 1–2). Similarly, at the 1848 Seneca Falls Conference that defined the suffrage movement, Elizabeth Cady Stanton issued the "Declaration of Sentiments." She began, "We hold these truths to be self-evident; that all men and women are created equal; that they are endowed by their Creator with certain inalienable rights; that among these are life, liberty, and the pursuit of happiness" (Stanton, 1889, p. 70).

Similarities exist in the content of abolitionist and suffragist claims, as well as in the freedom fighters' strategies. In the "Declaration of Sentiments," Stanton listed 18 grievances (the same number contained in the Declaration of Independence), many of which characterized Black oppression as well the oppression of women. Among these grievances were the prohibition on voting, lack of access to higher education, and inability to work in respected professions such as medicine and law. The employment of both Black people and women was generally confined to menial and severely underpaid or free labor. Moreover, earnings, if any, belonged to the masters of the house, who had the authority to beat their wives and slaves with impunity. Stanton also recognized the power of internalized oppression. Among the grievances listed in the "Declaration of Sentiments" was the man's endeavor "to destroy [the woman's] confidence in her own powers, to lessen her self-respect, and to make her willing to lead a dependent and abject life" (Stanton, 1889, p. 71). Interestingly, all the resolutions outlined by Stanton were approved unanimously at the Seneca Falls Convention, except for the highly controversial right to vote, which passed narrowly only after an appeal by Frederick Douglass (Schneir, 1972).

Although there are numerous similarities between the Black freedom movements and women's rights movements, important differences exist as well. These differences are of vital significance for children's rights. The remainder of this section examines three features of the women's movement with implications for children's rights: the need to uncover oppression within one's most intimate (and even loving) relationships; the need to resist relegation to the home; and the importance of separating physical strength from moral superiority.

In the 1960s, and even today, White people could, and many did, engineer their lives so as to rarely encounter Black people. The notion that Black and White people could be "separate but equal" appealed to many. With regard to gender, however, such segregation was neither possible nor desirable. Men and women lived under the same roof, dined together, had children together, and worshipped together.

For women, at least for the influential White women in the second wave of the women's movement, disenfranchisement from civic life stemmed from their relegation to the home. The women's movement demonstrated that inequality occurs in both public *and* private spheres, in relation to people with whom we interact minimally and people with whom we share the most intimate aspects of our lives. At the same time that women fought for the right to participate in civic life, they also sought to transform their private lives, to redefine the smallest democracy— the democracy of the family. The Black civil rights movement was waged largely in public spaces—communities of Black people who organized in churches and took their often large-scale protests to the streets, to the buses, and to businesses. Women's consciousness-raising occurred among small groups of friends gathered together around kitchen tables. Their messages initially were designed for the individual men with whom they lived most closely. The women's movement made clear that "the personal is political."

Confinement to the home has rendered both women and children invisible (e.g., Oakley, 1994). Beginning in the 1960s, however, women began to participate more actively in civic life. In 1963, the controversial and bestselling book *The Feminine Mystique,* by Betty Friedan, exposed and countered the prevailing myth that women achieved personal fulfillment in the private sphere of the home. The book gave voice to the unrest and dissatisfaction that countless women suffered in isolation and helped make the women's movement necessary. Before long, women began to organize. While many of the grievances voiced by pioneers of the women's movement in Seneca Falls remained on the political agenda of women's rights activists of the 1960s, new concerns arose. These were more intimate concerns, such as women's health care, reproductive rights, domestic violence, and rape. The new concerns of the women's movement of the 1960s highlighted the private nature of women's oppression. These concerns also made clear the <u>ways in which disparities in physical strength can fuel oppression.</u>

In a country that attempts to coerce democracy through military power, it is not surprising that might often is confused with right. Throughout history, sporting events have served as arenas in which to test both physical and moral superiority. Illusions of White men's greatness came crashing down in boxing matches that pitted White fighters against Black fighters like Jack Johnson, Joe Louis, and Muhammad Ali. To this day, and despite the fact that boxing has never been of any interest to me, I remember standing on line in the hallway of my elementary school arguing with peers about whether Muhammad Ali would prove himself to be "The Greatest." Even at that young age, my classmates and I knew that our opinions were based not on any knowledge of boxing, but on our ideas about social equality.

The tennis match between Billie Jean King and Bobby Riggs brought national attention to women's rights just as interracial boxing championships became battlegrounds for civil rights. However, tying the equality of women to the outcomes of sporting events is exceedingly dangerous. Although Billie Jean King proved victorious, Bobby Riggs was hardly in his prime at the time of their match. Men, as a group, are undeniably more physically powerful than women. And both men and women can physically overpower a young child with ease.

The ways in which physical strength can perpetuate oppression struck me one morning while watching cartoons with my sons. One of the joys of parenthood is the opportunity to relive childhood pleasures alongside one's children. Parents look forward to sharing books, movies, and television shows that we remember fondly from our own childhoods. A sign of social progress is that some scenes that went unremarked on in our own childhoods jar us when encountered today.

As a child I admired Penelope Pitstop, the sole female racer and occasional winner in the otherwise male cartoon cast of *Wacky Races*. Despite being a diminutive woman, Penelope Pitstop could challenge men on the racetrack. Decades later, however, while sitting beside my car-loving sons, I watched with embarrassment as Penelope Pitstop pushed the buttons on the control panel of her car, the "Compact Pussycat," that enabled her to apply lipstick, dry her hair (despite the fact that it lay largely covered by her helmet), and even vibrate away excess fat all while she drove.

A forgotten scene in the cartoon *Speed Racer* left me appalled rather than embarrassed. Trixie, the beautiful young woman who assisted Speed in his racing career, was a woman ahead of her time. She could pilot a helicopter, decode secret messages, and save the day. But in one scene, Speed and his mechanic friend struggled to fix the racecar while Trixie insisted that Speed rest after a life-threatening ordeal. The mechanic complained about Trixie and so Speed ended the discussion by lifting her off the ground and carrying her, kicking and screaming, back to her helicopter. It seemed to me an assault on her humanity. Then I had one of those uncomfortable stutters in my flowing and unthinking narrative—a rending of the fabric of my everyday experience. I thought of the ease with which adults lift and carry protesting children, and recognized that this option exists because of the adult's greater physical strength, not as a result of moral superiority.

In many ways, women's rights have progressed further than children's rights. Most women are no longer segregated from civic life by their relegation to the home. Children, however, continue to exist primarily within the private sphere of the family, where their treatment is impervious to public scrutiny except in extreme circumstances. In addition, there is increasing social disapproval for the use of physical force against women in the United States, but physical force against children remains sanctioned. It is illegal in all 50 states for an adult to strike any other adult, but all 50 states allow the corporal punishment of children by adults.

Unfortunately, some of women's advances since the 1960s have come at the expense of children. The women's movement emphasized the importance of reproductive freedom and economic independence. Thus, freedom and independence *for* women often meant freedom *from* children. A feminist in the second wave of the women's movement, Shulamith Firestone, foresaw this separation of women's rights from children's rights and tried to counter it. In her classic 1972 book, *Dialectics of Sex,* she considered who should speak on behalf of children and concluded, "It is up to feminist (ex-children and still oppressed child-women) revolutionaries to do so." Firestone argued that even though "many women are sick and tired of being lumped together with children," there has developed, "in our long period of related sufferings, a certain compassion and understanding for them that there is no reason to lose now" (pp. 101–102 in the original, cited in Oakley, 1994, p. 31).

Since the 1960s, women have gained the rights to vote, to own property, to receive an education, and to join elite professions. As a result, their position in society has improved. The children's rights movement, however, cannot depend on similar achievements for children. Children most likely will not become voters, homeowners, or lawyers. Children cannot live independent from adults. How can civil rights exist alongside dependence on others? Some answers may be found in another rights movement, the movement of people with disabilities.

Learning from the Disability Rights Movement: "Nothing About Us Without Us"

The disability rights movement has profound implications for children's rights. This section discusses two: the need to value human connectedness and interdependence as well as autonomy, and the role of fostering participation through altering the physical environment so that access to both public and private spaces exists.

The first objection to the notion of children's civil rights often pertains to children's relative immaturity—their physical, intellectual, emotional, and even moral limitations. The implication is that children are *not* equal to adults and so should not have the same rights. One might argue, however, that children's vulnerability increases rather than decreases the onus on adults to safeguard their civil rights. In a 2001 address, the disability rights activist Tom Shakespeare made a similar claim with regard to people with disabilities. He noted that people with impairments "don't only have a set of discriminations and prejudices to fight against, you have issues of body and brain to deal with too, for which you need proper support and proper services."

The same could be said of children whose struggle for rights is complicated not by their impairment, but by their tender age. Children, too, might be said to bear the burdens not only of discrimination and prejudice, but also of differences in their bodies and brains that necessitate additional support rather than sanction from the adults with whom they share their lives. Just as Shakespeare believed in simultaneously "supporting the civil rights of disabled people while seeking to reduce the impact of impairment and illness," we might support children's rights while simultaneously fostering their growth. Indeed, optimal development may depend on adults honoring, from the moment of birth, children's rights as humans and as citizens.

It seems useful to draw a distinction here between inherent vulnerability and structural vulnerability (Lansdown, 1994). Some of children's dependence on adults results from their inherent vulnerability, which includes their physical weakness, small stature, and lack of experience as compared with adults. But structural vulnerability further limits children's participation. That is, "Children are also vulnerable because of their complete lack of political and economic power and their lack of civil rights in our society" (Lansdown, 1994, p. 34). The existence of inherent vulnerability does not justify the support of structural vulnerability.

The disability rights movement only recently has acknowledged that impairment matters. Understandably, in a culture of rugged individualism, proponents of disability rights initially downplayed disabled citizens' need for assistance. Indeed, in the late 1960s the disability rights movement became synonymous with the movement for *independent living*. This was an understandable but unfortunate misnomer. "Independent living" meant that people with disabilities should not be separated from society through institutionalization, but should receive the support and services required for them to live in the community with a home, a job, a place of worship, and so on. Disability rights are, therefore, not about independence, but about *assisted participation*. People with disabilities may need to be *assisted* in order to realize the goal of *participation*. The importance of assisted participation lies at the heart of the rallying cry of disability rights activists, "Nothing About Us Without Us."

Children also require assistance in realizing their right to participation. There are activities that children cannot do on their own and that require adult support. Consider, for example, this entry to the Boulder Journey School Charter on Children's Rights (see Chapter 1): "Children have a right to know what time it is, and how many minutes they have to wait for something (their turn), and the time it will be when it's finally their turn."

The rights movement of the 1960s and early 1970s did not challenge the cultural value placed on self-determination and autonomy. In the late 1970s and 1980s, however, activists, especially women activists, began to consider the importance of interdependence. The psychologist Carol Gilligan (1982), for example, challenged Lawrence Kohlberg's (1981) emphasis on rationality and justice as the basis of moral reasoning. She argued for the relevance of relationships and caring as well.

Both the disability rights movement and the children's rights movement need to recast the discourse on rights as a balance between independence and connectedness. Embracing interdependence does not mean, however, fostering dependence. Neither people with disabilities nor children benefit when others presume to do for them what they are capable of doing for themselves.

In addition to challenging the view of independence and self-sufficiency as the ultimate goal of development and measure of worth, a second lesson for children's rights from the disabilities rights movement is the need to foster participation through alterations in the physical environment. Although able-bodied people usually view disabilities as residing within the disabled person, activists have proposed that *environments* handicap people (e.g., Fine & Asch, 1988). For example, deafness would pose fewer limitations in a community where everyone used sign language. The effort to transform physical environments has driven many important court battles in the struggle for disability rights. The landmark Americans with Disabilities Act of 1990 has numerous provisions to prevent discrimination in employment, housing, and other arenas, but its most visible effect is the transformation of the environment: lowered curbs, wheelchair- accessible bathrooms, elevators, and close-by parking.

It is interesting to ponder how a children's act, similar to the Americans with Disabilities Act, would transform the physical spaces that exclude children in our own communities, indeed, in our own homes. Preliminary ideas might be found in classroom spaces designed to encourage children's participation in school life, notably environments influenced by the work of educators in Reggio Emilia. Mirrors, supplies, sinks, and cupboards might be placed at a child's level, and stepstools might be available for children to reach high places. Low ballet bars in hallways can support young toddlers who are learning to walk. The entrances to play and sleeping areas might be lowered so that children could come and go on their own, and steps would allow mobile children to climb onto and off of changing tables on their own (see Goldschmeid & Jackson, 1994).

When my younger son was 2, he began to carry a small wooden stool from room to room so he could more easily reach refrigerators, sinks, and cabinets. No one else, not even his beloved big brother, was allowed on the stool. This initially seemed "cute," but one day, when he couldn't reach his stool, the expression I saw flash across his face brought back the feeling I had when I awoke and couldn't feel my glasses on the nightstand. My glasses and my son's stool were instruments for participation in the world. Without them we both felt, I think, acutely vulnerable.

In addition to structural changes in the environment, tools that small bodies can use also facilitate children's participation. Maria Montessori pioneered the creation of child-sized tools that actually worked (see Mooney, 2000), rather than ineffective, plastic facsimiles that undermine a child's sense of competence. In the past few years, supermarkets have begun to provide not only shopping carts designed to look like cars and trucks that children can pretend to drive, but also small carts that allow children to shop themselves.

When adults prepare for the arrival of children, considerable time and effort is spent in *childproofing*: the installation of toilet locks, outlet covers, safety gates, and so on. Adults concentrate on creating barriers to protect children. Perhaps the time has come to devote commensurate attention to *child-promoting*. How can adults facilitate children's participation in the world around them at home, at school, and beyond?

CONCLUSION

> *We are the children of the world, and despite our different backgrounds, we share a common reality.*
> *We are united by our struggle to make the world a better place for all.*
> *You call us the future, but we are also the present.*
>   —Thirteen-year-old Gabriela Azurduy Arrieta from Bolivia and
>   17-year-old Audrey Cheynut from Monaco, 2002 representatives of the
>   Children's Forum (in address to the United Nations Special Session on Children)

This chapter has explored numerous ways in which the marginalization of children in the United States parallels the marginalization of other groups and has outlined lessons children's rights activists might glean from other social movements. One additional lesson is the need to recognize that people have multiple identities. The Black civil rights movement did not always value the contributions of women, while the women's movement neglected the concerns of women of color. Children are not only children; they also have a gender, race, disability/ability status, national origin, and so on. Thus, the nature of the challenges children face in their society depends not only on their status as children but on other statuses as well.

Despite the heterogeneity of the social group "children," a common denominator in their struggle for rights is the need for adult allies to amplify their voices. As described in the previous chapter, this requires a new pedagogy of listening on the part of adults.

We believe that the civic participation of children is essential not only for their well-being, but also in the hope of creating more just, humane, and inclusive social arrangements in the home, in the classroom, and in the larger society. It would be enough to commit to children's rights because it is the right thing to do, because it honors the humanity of the children in our lives. But a commitment to children's rights accomplishes much more. A transformation of power relationships between children and adults can provide a model for negotiating relationships across other differences in status that too easily become the basis for social inequity. As adults and children work to find new ways of relating to each other, so too may we find new ways of relating across differences in race, gender, disability/ability status, socioeconomic status, religion, and nationality.

In an essay entitled "Learning from the 60s," the activist poet Audre Lorde (1984) noted the links among antipoor policies, desecration of synagogues, and violence against African Americans, women, and gay people. Lorde (1984) wrote, "I ask myself as well as each one of you, exactly what alteration in the social fabric of my everyday life does this connection call for?" (p. 139). This chapter examined some of the alterations in the social fabric of daily life required by linking children's rights with other rights movements.

Change does not come easy, but it is possible. When children initiate new conversations that leave adults stuttering, they offer us priceless opportunities to create change with them. Struggles for civil rights have shown that quests for freedom do not begin in vast social movements, but in the hearts and minds of individuals (Harding, 1990). By altering the fabric of our daily lives with children, we help create the democratic ideal on which our country was founded. We owe it to the children of tomorrow, the children of today, and the children of yesterday. Which is to say, we owe it to us all.

For Further Thought

1. Discuss the idea of assisted participation as it pertains to children. Give examples of activities that children cannot do on their own and require adult support. How do you offer support in a way that respects the child's rights?
2. Based on your observations of children's environments, describe possible adaptations to homes/schools/communities that would make these environments more child-promoting. Go to a setting you visit with children and sketch out alterations you might make to this environment to make it more child-friendly. Bring a child or group of children with you and invite them to draw pictures of what they do and do not like about the environment, as well as what they wish the environment would offer them.
3. Recall a time when you picked up a protesting child. Describe the occurrence, how you felt, and what other options you might have chosen.

NOTE

1. In November 2009, Somalia signaled its intent to ratify the UNCRC, but the country is unable to proceed in doing so because it currently has no recognized government. See http://www.unicef.org/crc/index_30229.html.

CHAPTER 3

The Special Estate of Children's Rights: A Movement Like No Other

Chapter 2 explored parallels between a children's rights movement and other movements for human rights. The authors discussed, for example, how members of *all* marginalized groups struggle with invisibility and internalized oppression, and how liberation efforts benefit from attention to the gaps between rhetoric (how one believes people should be treated) and reality (how one actually treats members of marginalized groups). In Chapter 2 we also outlined points of intersection between specific rights movements. For example, both children's and women's liberation must address disparities in physical strength and relegation to the home. In this chapter, we approach children's rights from the opposite direction: the ways in which children's rights are unique and why a children's rights movement must be a movement like no other.

Some activists hold that the struggle for children's liberation completely parallels the struggles of other groups. Richard Farson (1974) argued that the heart of any rights movement is the right to self-determination and that "children, like adults, should have a right to decide the matters which affect them most directly" (p. 27). Farson examined children's right to self-determination in different arenas, such as education, economics, politics, and law. Although Farson presented provocative challenges to common conceptions of children's rights, the limits to his argument are apparent to the authors of this book in his proposal that "sexual experimentation and sexual acts between consenting people [regardless of age] can be enjoyed without fear of punishment" (pp. 152–153). The authors wholeheartedly disagree with this recommendation.

Farson's belief in children's self-determination without limits stands in contrast to child advocates who favor protection over participation. In *The Hurried Child*, David Elkind (1988) objected to the pressures for children to grow up too fast and envisioned childhood as a sheltered space. He called for strict limits on children's self-determination, arguing that it is age-appropriate to ask children what they want for dinner, but not appropriate to ask with which parent they want to share a holiday. The authors of this book also disagree with this recommendation. As stated in Article 12 of the United Nations Convention on the Rights of the

Child (Office of the United Nations High Commission for Human Rights, 1989), children should have a voice in "all matters affecting the child."

In this chapter we explore the ground between the positions of Farson and Elkind. We do not believe that children should be entrusted with decisions about having sex with adults (indeed, not all adults can be trusted with such decisions!). We do believe, however, that children's viewpoints *always* matter and that children should have a voice in decisions far more important than what to have for dinner. Having a voice is not the same as deciding a matter. Confusing the two hinders the advancement of children's rights. As the child rights researcher Priscilla Alderson (2000b) stated, if "participation is taken to mean children's rights 'to do whatever they want,' 'to divorce their parents' or 'to refuse to go to school or have life-saving medical treatment' then all participation, even expressing a view or being informed, is easily dismissed as dangerous nonsense" (p. 114). To say that children have a right to express an opinion means that children should be able to influence decisions, *not* that their decisions must automatically be endorsed.

BALANCING PROTECTION AND PARTICIPATION

Advancing children's rights requires a careful and conscious balancing of children's protection *and* participation rights. In the United States adult caretakers experience enormous pressure to protect children at all costs. Adults are faulted for a failure to protect but not for a failure to allow. The authors propose that in order to advance children's rights adults must make spaces for children as safe as *necessary* rather than as safe as *possible* (H. Nebelong, personal communication, October 17, 2006).

Making spaces as safe as *necessary* means assessing risk realistically. As a country we recently have worried over imminent crises that never materialized, such as SARS, anthrax, and West Nile virus. Assertive advocacy groups, ambitious politicians, and sensationalistic media promote unrealistic fears, while an opportunistic legal system stands ready to capitalize on unfortunate accidents. Real risks exist, but they are often far less than adults believe. Even when school shootings seemed to occur everywhere, Americans faced a far greater risk of being struck by lightning than falling to school violence (see Glassner, 2000; Siegel, 2005).

Making spaces as safe as necessary means recognizing that overprotection entails risks as well. As Helen Keller (1957) observed:

> Security is mostly a superstition. It does not exist in nature, nor do the children of man as a whole experience it. . . . Avoiding danger is no safer in the long run than outright exposure. . . . Life is either a daring adventure or nothing. (p. 17)

Adults' desire to protect can deprive children of their right to participation. The current generation of children spends less and less time out of the home and in unsupervised play (Lansdown, 1994). A study in London found that in 1971, 80%

of 7- and 8-year-olds were allowed to travel to school alone, but by 1990 only 9% traveled alone (M. Hillman, Adams, & Whitelegg, 1991). The statistics for children in the United States are most likely comparable. Journalist and author Richard Louv (2005) observed, "Fear is the most potent force that prevents parents from allowing their children the freedom they themselves enjoyed when they were young" (p. 123).

Overprotection prevents children from engaging with the world around them. This is evident in the popular children's movie *Finding Nemo* (2003), which opens with a predator fish devouring the mother clownfish and all but one of her spawn. Only the egg containing Nemo survives. The father clownfish, Marlin, promises his only surviving child, "I'll never let anything happen to you." Marlin fails in this effort and during an attempt to rescue his son; he recounts his broken promise to Dory, a ditzy but wise blue tang. Dory responds, "Well, you can't never let anything happen to him. Then nothing would ever happen to him."

Adults cannot and perhaps should not try to keep anything from ever happening to our children. As one developmental theorist asserted, children today need more "smells, tastes, splinters, and accidents" (cited in Nabhan & Trimble, 1994, p. 9). Exuberance characterizes childhood. "Scrubbing and polishing raw experience in the name of health and safety scrapes away the natural luster and meaning of childhood" (Greenman, 2005b, p. 7).

Not all countries put a similar emphasis on protection. In Sweden, school grounds might flow into surrounding natural environments, and children can choose to play away from the watchful eyes of adults. Injuries occur, but "the cost of a broken arm was to be measured against the child's right to play freely with other children" (Moss & Petrie, 2002, p. 129).

Although children sometimes make dangerous choices (as adults sometimes do), educators at Boulder Journey School more often are struck by children's sound judgment. One teacher asked a 4-year-old child to photograph anything in the school playground that he thought dangerous or unsafe. When the teacher and child discussed his photographs, the teacher realized that the boy wisely viewed danger as tied to behaviors rather than to objects. He did not assert that the climber was an unsafe place but that jumping from it was an unsafe act. Moreover, remarkable similarities emerged between this boy's viewpoint and the ideas expressed by a fellow teacher, as depicted in Figure 3.1 (Mooreshead, 2006).

The young boy, listening to his teacher's responses, also was struck by the similarity in their perspectives, commenting, "Yeah, that's what I said!" At Boulder Journey School, teachers and children alike talk about safety in terms of taking responsibility for one's actions, not about making the equipment so safe that it offers few physical challenges.

The authors have wondered together about the benefits of providing young children with opportunities to practice decision making in the context of small risks. Allowing small risks may develop trust between adults and children. Furthermore, if children have the freedom to explore the parameters of their competencies in childhood, they may be less likely to court larger risks in the future. In

FIGURE 3.1. Remarkable similarities emerge between a child's viewpoints and the ideas expressed by his teacher.

Equipment	Child's Comments	Teacher's Comments
Monkey Bars	Don't do it if you're little. Don't do it if you don't want to do it. But do do it if you do.	I feel like after age three if they feel like they are ready, then they are probably ready.
Top of the Climber	If you jump from there it's dangerous. You can get hurt.	I think it's a natural exploration to want to jump. . . . But if it's from the highest point I get a little nervous when they jump from the top of the climber. I fear broken bones.

Finding Nemo, Marlin attempted to make his son's world as safe as possible, to protect Nemo from all imaginable risks. When the young clownfish began to grow into independence, however, he decided to take a very great risk that almost cost both Nemo and Marlin their lives. In the United States, where adults generally favor the protection rather than the participation of young children, many battles between adults and adolescents center on the adolescents' newfound freedom and ability to take risks. Unfortunately, in the teenage years the consequences of poor choices have outcomes far more serious than a broken arm. Might adolescents' willingness to abuse substances, engage in risky sex, or drive dangerously reflect a desire to escape from the adult protections they have long deemed oppressive?

Adults' will to protect does not generally arise from malevolent intent. As we will discuss later in this chapter, the special love of adults for children can constrain as well as enable. It also seems possible that protecting children is a way for adults to live vicariously in a world without pain. Children live with both physical and emotional vulnerability. They greet the world around them with open hearts. They have not yet learned to protect themselves with emotional barriers that keep pain, disappointment, and broken dreams at a distance. Indeed, it may be this openness that allows children to so readily forgive the adults in their lives, no matter how badly *we* behave.

The immediacy of children's experience, their "innocence," can intensify adults' desire to shelter children from the harshness of the world. Children do not always, however, want to be denied participation in painful realities. As the constructors of the Boulder Journey School Charter on Children's Rights asserted, "Children have a right to pretend being dead and think about what it means to be dead" (see Chapter 1). When adults protect children, we also protect ourselves. In order to truly be with children in the present, to accompany them in their raw experience of fear, pain, or injustice, adults must break down the walls that protect our own hearts.

The popular image of the child as an innocent living in a golden age of carefree play and sunshine necessitates a protected space separate from the "real" world of adulthood. Sentimentalized visions of childhood, however, deny the reality of children's experience. Jim Greenman (2005a) asserted, "It is one thing to create a sanctuary for children . . . for a few hours a day where they spend much of their days and weeks in the world, with parents and others. It is quite another when that sanctuary is nearly all of the world they experience directly" (p. 31). The authors have found that in most instances, children do not seek to be shielded from the activities of adults, and instead wish to be acknowledged as contributors within their communities.

Certainly adults *do* need to protect children's physical and emotional well-being, especially in times of heightened vulnerability from factors such as compromised health or social upheaval. At the same time, adults need to respect and cultivate children's competence and their engagement with the world around them. Protection cannot be a justification for refusing children their rights to participation.

THE UNIQUE STATUS OF CHILDREN

Elkind (1988) recognized that "the trend toward obscuring the divisions between children and adults is part of a broad egalitarian movement in this country that seeks to overcome the barriers separating the sexes, ethnic and racial groups, and the handicapped" (p. 21). Unlike Farson, however, Elkind believed that children's liberation should *not* fall under the rubric of larger egalitarian movements. Elkind applauded the movements for the rights of women, for ethnic and racial groups, and for people with disabilities, but asserted:

> Its unthinking extension to children is unfortunate. . . . Children need time to grow, to learn, and to develop. To treat them differently from adults is not to discriminate against them but rather to recognize their special estate. (p. 21)

One could argue, however, that *all* oppressed groups have "special estate" due to their unique vulnerabilities. Liberation means the promotion of equitable, but not necessarily equivalent, treatment. As a society, policymakers sometimes attempt to achieve egalitarian goals through *unequal* treatment. Reserved parking spaces and ramps exist to facilitate the equal access of physically handicapped people, and affirmative action sought to rectify a history of inequality by actively recruiting underrepresented minorities into schools and the workplace.

In this chapter we examine four aspects of childhood's "special estate," that is, four ways in which the status of "child" is a unique status. First, "child" is a social group that *everyone* belongs to at some time. Second, adults and children have different bodies and minds. Third, adults have more life experience than children. Fourth, children and adults exist in a relationship of "loving interdependence." All of these unique aspects of being a child have profound implications for a children's rights movement.

Everyone Is or Has Been a Child

For many of the social statuses according to which society apportions privilege, individuals are either in one camp or the other. Most people easily can be classified as either male or female, for example. Although increasing numbers of biracial and multiracial people challenge the dichotomy of White and non-White, race membership, like gender, is usually lifelong and immutable. Other statuses, such as socioeconomic status and ability/disability status, are more fluid, but boundary-crossing is not inevitable. Children as a class of people differ from all other marginalized classes in that every one of us either is or once was a child. One might think that a firsthand experience of childhood would increase adults' sensitivity to children's marginalization. The contrary, however, often seems to occur.

Research supports the notion that we recreate as parents what we experienced as children. The psychiatrist John Bowlby (1973/1980) theorized that beginning in infancy, interactions with parents and other important caregivers result in a set of beliefs and expectations about how relationships work, or "internal working models of relationships." In childhood we learn from our caregivers how to love, care for, and attend to others. We also learn the intricacies of ill treatment—how to silence, hurt, and control.

Despite the best of intentions, many adults unwittingly reproduce with their own children harmful dynamics from their early lives. As an extreme example, people who abuse children are likely to have experienced abuse in their own childhoods. Less obvious forms of maltreatment also cross generations. Avi Assor and his colleagues (2004) studied people who believed that their parents loved them only when they fulfilled parental expectations. Study participants acknowledged the damage that such conditional love caused in their own lives, but nevertheless admitted to using identical parenting strategies with their children (reported in *Unconditional Parenting* by Alfie Kohn, 2005). As a more common example of reproducing unpleasant childhood dynamics, many of us have heard with shock and dismay our own parents' voices emerging from our throats, as when we silence our children with such pronouncements as, "Because I said so," or "Because I'm your mother/father."

In her book, *All About Love,* the social critic bell hooks (2000) noted that in most childhoods, maltreatment and "love" co-exist. Some people even come to understand abuse as an expression of "love." She contended that an unwillingness to come to terms with the lack of love in one's past prevents adults from behaving differently with their children. Similarly, the psychoanalyst Alice Miller (1983) held that injustices cross generations because maltreatment represents people's struggles "to regain the power once lost to their own parents" (p. 16). In this regard, the phenomenon of hazing offers a parallel: Someone in a less powerful group undergoes mistreatment as a rite of passage into the more powerful group, and when advanced to a position of power, inflicts the same mistreatment on less powerful others. There is, however, cause for optimism about ending the transmission of maltreatment across generations. Although children who experience abuse at the hands of their parents face a greater risk of abusing their own children, the majority do *not* become abusers (Miller & Challas, 1980; Oliver, 1993).

Adults are not alone in asserting power based on age. Children also seek to position themselves above those who are younger, perhaps wielding the cutting insult, "You're just a baby." The authors suspect that adults' valuing of maturity helps justify older children's assertions of power over younger children. Although celebrating achievement is important, we have wondered about the subtext of messages praising children with reference to how big they are getting. "You're so big now, you can feed yourself/use the potty/ not cry when your parents leave/ tie your shoes/sit through a religious service." In bestowing such praise, do adults imply that bigger (older) is better? Do we convey that the child has become better than she or he was before? Does such praise suggest that the older child is superior to younger children who cannot yet do those things? And while we're posing questions, doesn't it seem that adults often praise "bigness" when the child has succeeded in doing something that makes *adult* lives easier? To the extent that this kind of praise feeds young people's fever to grow up as fast as possible, we echo Elkind's call to stop hurrying children.

Children are surrounded by messages that being bigger/older is better, and they certainly see that adults have more decision-making power. When other marginalized groups witness similar disparities in power, however, they do not generally wish to join the more powerful group. Women do not aspire to become men, nor do Black people aspire to be White, or deaf people to hear. Layered onto the perception of adulthood as superior to childhood is the knowledge of the temporariness of childhood. Many adults (and children) view childhood as a state of "adulthood in waiting" (Moss & Petrie, 2002; see also Farson, 1974). As a result, children may be seen not as human *beings,* but rather as human *becomings* (Alderson, 2000b; Quortrup, 1987; see also Phillips & Alderson, 2002) who are not yet full participants in society.

If children matter only in the future, they remain invisible in the present. The temporariness of childhood reduces the urgency with which adults and children alike seek to eliminate age-based inequality. Janusz Korczak (n.d.), an advocate for children's rights who perished in a concentration camp along with the 200 orphans in his care, advised, "Children are not people of tomorrow, they're people of today." Our caring and respect for children *as children* must drive the struggle for children's rights.

Adults and Children Have Different Bodies and Minds

Elkind (1988) posited that developmental differences between children and adults legitimated and necessitated greater self-determination rights for adults. The authors agree that age differences exist in many domains—physical, cognitive, emotional, social. At the same time, we do not unquestioningly accept accumulated wisdom about the exact nature of these differences. In our own work we find, for example, that the commonly held notion in developmental psychology that young children cannot take the perspectives of others is wrong. No one can know the capabilities of children until the images of children that we hold as individuals, and as a society, serve to inspire rather than stifle children's thoughts and actions.

William Ryan (1971) astutely observed in his classic book *Blaming the Victim* that oppression first requires the identification of differences between members of the dominant group and members of the marginalized group. Next, the dominant group is held as the standard, and the marginalized group members are found lacking in comparison. Members of marginalized groups are not simply different, but inferior. Thus, for example, women's interest in caretaking may be labeled "codependent," and involvement of extended family in child rearing among African American families viewed as a symptom of "family disintegration."

In addition, systems of oppression constrain behavioral options so that members of marginalized groups cannot help but behave in ways deemed problematic. For example, bell hooks (2000) observed that the opinions and beliefs of women often are devalued. Thus, "one reason women traditionally gossiped more than men is because gossip has been a social interaction wherein women have felt comfortable stating what they really think and feel" (p. 59).

For evidence of negative images of children, one need look no further than the word "childish." Synonyms of this word include immature, irresponsible, silly, self-indulgent, and foolish. Resistance to children's oppression requires that adults question whether children have these "childish" attributes at all, and, if they do, consider the adult's role in creating the very behaviors that are denounced. Maria Montessori (1967) observed that "the weeping, the shouting, the tantrums, the timidity, the possessiveness, the fibs, the selfishness and spirit of destruction" might best be understood as "only the efforts and the energy that are necessary for the child to defend itself against us" (p. 7). More recently, professor of childhood studies Berry Mayall (2000b) stated, "Children's own subordination to adults leads them to adopt whatever tactics they can in order to assert their rights; these tactics, which include wheedling, lying, demanding, refusing, themselves reinforce adult prejudices" (p. 137).

A respectful consideration of adult–child differences requires that adults attempt to cast aside adult-centric lenses that distort children's behavior to fit prevalent assumptions about children's inferiority. The authors attempt to do this in the following sections, which consider differences in both bodies and minds.

Differences in Bodies: Physical Size and Strength. Perhaps the least controvertible statement one can make about adult–child differences is that adults are physically bigger and stronger. Previous chapters have suggested some implications of children's smaller stature for children's rights. Much of children's exclusion from the adult world results from their lesser size and strength. Simply altering the physical environment to accommodate children's stature would greatly facilitate their meaningful participation, just as attempts to make environments wheelchair accessible have expanded the social participation of people with physical handicaps.

Children, more often than adults, lack the size and strength to achieve a goal independently. In this culture of rugged individualism, the inability to accomplish a task on one's own easily translates into weakness and inferiority. A different worldview might lead us to view the inability to accomplish a task on one's own as an opportunity for collaboration. Teachers at Boulder Journey School documented, on video, the efforts of a group of children determined to transport a very large pumpkin from the garden to the classroom in order to carve it into a jack o' lantern. Viewers of this video tend *not* to focus on the weakness of the children, but appreciate instead their joint problem-solving and collaborative efforts. Together the children achieved a feat akin to a community barn raising. Instances of children's collaboration, as seen in Figure 3.2, occur frequently when children problem-solve together.

In order for children to succeed in transporting a pumpkin or moving in a wagon, adults need to resist taking over. Assumptions of weakness can compel "helping" when help is neither required nor appreciated. Indeed, "help" sometimes can be counterproductive. Research shows that unwanted assistance and overly solicitous attention from relatives hinders recovery from illnesses and accidents (Glass, Matchar, Belyea, & Feussner, 1993; Wortman & Lehman, 1985). Shirley Kleinman, the mother of Ellen Hall (one of this book's authors), elaborated on many of these frustrations in a book she wrote after surviving a stroke (Kleinman & Menn, 1997). "Helping" may make helpers feel useful. It also can be expedient. But savings in time may occur at a cost to the sense of mastery and autonomy in the recipient of help.

Differences in Minds: Divergent and Convergent Thinking. Brain imaging has revealed that when children perform word tasks, they activate more regions of their brains than do adults. Such brain images offer convincing evidence that adults and children think differently. Questions remain, however, as to what meanings to attach to observed differences. The researchers who made this discovery framed the differences in brain activity as a shortcoming in children, proposing that people make more efficient use of their brains as they mature (reported in Giese, 2008). Alternatively, we might entertain the child-centric explanation that young people evidence less rigidity in their thinking.

Reggio Emilia scholar Carlina Rinaldi (2006) observed that young children easily combine unusual elements in their thinking. Adults find this difficult to do for several reasons:

> First of all, because convergent thinking is convenient, but also because changing your mind often represents a loss of power. Children, on the other hand, search for power by changing their minds, in the honesty that they have toward ideas and toward others, in their honesty of listening. But they quickly understand that having ideas that diverge from those of their teachers or their parents and expressing them at the wrong moment is not a positive thing. (Rinaldi, 2006, p. 118)

As seen in Chapter 1, children's flexibility in thinking characterizes their use of language. Reggio Emilia pedagogista and philosopher Loris Malaguzzi coined

FIGURE 3.2. Instances of children's collaboration occur frequently when children problem solve together. © Boulder Journey School, 2010.

the term *100 languages* to convey his respect for children's creativity and flexibility in constructing, representing, and expressing their ideas. Malaguzzi believed that children's flexibility "comes about because they have the privilege of not being excessively attached to their own ideas, which they construct and reinvent continuously" (Edwards, Gandini, & Forman, 1998, p. 75). Perhaps no one has put this openness to others' perspectives better than a child at a school in Reggio Emilia who said, "Not everybody thinks the same. If somebody thinks like you, she's a nuisance" (Reggio Children, 1995, p. 48).

Adults Have More Life Experience

Differences in the brains of adults and children most likely are driven by life experience. One important result of adults' accumulated life experiences is that adults are better able to foresee consequences. Adults have had many opportunities to observe the results of choices they and others have made, and so have more information on which to assess situations, including situations that entail risk. The knowledge gleaned through experience can inform adults' balancing of protection and participation, as discussed earlier in this chapter.

The authors believe that the challenge for adults is to utilize the knowledge gained through experience to help children negotiate childhood more productively, without removing opportunities for children to engage in the world around them and learn for themselves. Toward this goal, adults might try, when possible, to *offer* wisdom gained from experience rather than use life experience to justify control. When we offer instead of command, children maintain the power to refuse. Adults disallow children's opportunities to make decisions by either forbidding behaviors or turning probabilities into certainties. "If you don't get down from there you're going to fall." If the child should fall, adults might further assert their power (at the price of empathy) with the hard-to-resist, "I told you so."

Child rights researcher Priscilla Alderson (2000b) described a 14-month-old child's interest in touching a gas-fire tap. When the mother told the child not to touch it, the child seemed to realize that she could choose to cooperate or not. She touched the tap again and the mother firmly repeated her words. The child decided to defer to her mother's tone and look of concern. Alderson wrote, "These can be decisive moments when, in new ways, parents try pleading that can sound too weak, a force that is too strong, or else a kind of confident consulting, a direct appeal to the child's reason, sense and trust" (p. 44).

Lower-risk situations provide opportunities to offer children advice; for example, explaining the importance of taking the time to find mittens despite the call of newly fallen snow, or the reasonableness of going to the bathroom before getting into the car. While cold fingers and inconvenient bathroom stops are not fatal, higher-risk situations require firm limits on children's choices. Adults should not allow children to take a dip in the pool during a thunderstorm, for example. Adults can still, however, take the time to explain why a dip in the pool would be dangerous.

Respecting children's rights requires that adults assert control in measured ways and provide reasons for assertions of control. These explanations serve two equally important goals. First, when adults delineate the reasons for their use of power, we maximize the chances that children will learn from the adults' wealth of experience. Second, answering "why" questions holds adults accountable for their use of power. Sometimes adults do not have compelling reasons for their directives. A pause to consider "why" gives adults a chance to clarify their reasons to themselves as well as to the children. This opens the possibility for adults to realize that their constraints on children's decision making were not warranted. I have had to concede, for example, that pancakes for breakfast offer no nutritional advantage over chips and salsa. On a larger scale, pausing to question why children cannot vote compels the recognition that many (most?) adult voters are ill-informed and make decisions based on factors other than a clear and complete analysis of relevant issues.

The ability to foresee consequences allows adults to weigh the immediate risks of mittenless hands and swims during thunderstorms. Foresight also allows adults to balance the current wishes of a present-oriented child against the anticipated best interests of the future adult (e.g., Alderson, 1994). A child's present concern about the sting of an injection, for example, might overshadow that child's concern for her or his future health. This is not to say, however, that the perspective of children does not matter; their present concerns must be acknowledged and addressed as adults seek to protect children's putative future interests.

Adults and Children Have a Relationship of "Loving Interdependence"

One proponent of children's rights characterized the adult–child relationship as one of "loving interdependence" (Alderson, 1994, p. 50). Children are born dependent on adults and remain dependent for many years. This dependence distinguishes humans from most other animals. Fish, insects, and reptiles usually birth their offspring into complete self-sufficiency. Even large mammals evidence early autonomy. Baby deer and horses scramble onto their long legs within moments of their birth and soon can run with abandon. The prolonged dependence of human infants strengthens the social bonds between adults and children, but also creates a long-term and ever-shifting asymmetry of abilities that requires continual negotiation.

During a child's earliest years, adults spend much of their caretaking energy responding to physical states—the infant's need for food, warmth, physical contact, and hygiene. Perhaps this early focus on physical requirements contributes to the notion that adults fulfill parental obligations by providing for and protecting children's physical well-being. Indeed, some adults subscribe to the view that such caretaking absolves parents of responsibility for promoting children's self-determination. This can be seen, for example, in the parental decree, "As long as you live under my roof you will obey my rules."

Even after children become less dependent on parents for the fulfillment of physical needs, social dependence remains. Adults mediate between children and the social world beyond the family throughout childhood and into adolescence. As discussed in the previous chapter, children's relegation to the private sphere of the home gives parents near-exclusive power over children and removes children from political discourse (e.g., Moss & Petrie, 2002). In *The Hurried Child*, Elkind (1988) noted that children cannot vote, and do not have access to the media, and so need adults to advocate for them, as Elkind "tried to do in this book" (p. xv).

Although the authors share Elkind's dismay over children's lack of political clout, we do not believe that advocacy best ensures children's well-being. An advocate pleads the cause of another. We do not seek to speak *for* children but *with* them. We strive to be allies. Roger Hart (1994) developed the Ladder of Student Involvement (Figure 3.3) to distinguish different levels of children's involvement. The authors strive to stand as often as possible on the top rung, alongside the children in our lives.

Liberation theorists disagree about the extent to which people in the more powerful social group can truly ally with members of the marginalized group. As an illustration of the two schools of thought, Martin Luther King, Jr., believed that Black and White people could work together to achieve civil rights for Black people, whereas Malcolm X held that African Americans could gain liberation only through their own efforts (e.g., Cone, 1991). For children, however, there is no choice about whether to form an alliance with adults. Children's liberation requires collaboration between children and adults.

The activist/educator Paulo Freire (1970/1992) articulated the main barrier for a true alliance between dominant and marginalized group members: Powerful people do not want to forfeit their advantages and so tend to offer token concessions that actually maintain power differences. Fortunately, there is reason to believe that the special estate of childhood makes a true alliance between adults and children possible. There exists for adults in relationship with children a motivation for social change that may outweigh the desire to maintain power—the motivation of love.

The love of an adult for a child is like no other. As the cultural anthropologist Mary Catherine Bateson (2000) put it, "Children arrive like aliens from outer space, their needs and feelings inaccessible, sharing no common language, yet for all their strangeness we greet them with love" (p. 4). "Love" is a difficult word, an overused word with many layers of meaning. Kate Douglas Wiggin, founder of the first free West Coast kindergarten in 1878 and author of *Rebecca of Sunnybrook Farm,* decried mothers (although in today's society, fathers also might be implicated) who express love through indulgence. She wrote, "There are mothers who live in perfect puddles of maternal love, who yet seem incapable of justice; generous to a fault, perhaps, but seldom just" (Wiggin, 1892/2003, p. 4).

The love required for adults to ally with children in the pursuit of children's rights cannot flourish in puddles of provision or in prisons of protection. It requires a confluence of love and respect. The philosopher and educator David Hawkins (1997) held that "respect resembles love in its implicit aim of furtherance, but love without respect can blind and bind. Love is private and unbidden, whereas respect is implicit in all moral relations with others" (p. 350).

CONCLUSION

The status of "child" is unique for a variety of reasons. In this chapter, we have tried to show that children's qualities, such as their small statures, focus on the present, and dependence on adults, do not make children ineligible for participation rights. Instead of seeing adult–child differences as evidence of children's weakness, adults instead might view children as eager for collaboration, expansively creative, acutely sensitive to the world around them, and exquisitely forgiving. Indeed, children's flexible thinking, sense of wonder, and grounding in the present can provide a needed antidote to adult tendencies to become bogged down in financial worries, schedules, concerns about health, and other drudgeries of "the real world."

The meanings traditionally attached to the unique aspects of children's status have precluded adults from affording children their rights as citizens. The meanings are not, however, stagnant. As individuals and as a society we create "childhood" (e.g., Ariès, 1962; Heywood, 2001; Rinaldi, 2006), and this creation occurs over and over again, every day, around dining room tables and boardroom tables. The opportunity for children and adults to create new ways of being together exists everywhere, all the time. If children trust adults, they ask questions. If adults trust children, we ponder their questions with seriousness. In doing so, together we open the door to meaningful change.

FIGURE 3.3. The Ladder of Student Involvement in School (Hart, 1994). Reprinted with permission.

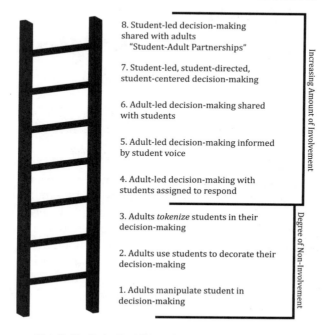

The Ladder of Student Involvement in School

8. Student-led decision-making
shared with adults
    "Student-Adult Partnerships"

7. Student-led, student-directed,
student-centered decision-making

6. Adult-led decision-making shared
with students

5. Adult-led decision-making informed
by student voice

4. Adult-led decision-making with
students assigned to respond

3. Adults *tokenize* students in their
decision-making

2. Adults use students to decorate their
decision-making

1. Adults manipulate student in
decision-making

Increasing Amount of Involvement

Degree of Non-Involvement

Adapted by Adam Fletcher (Freechild Project: http://www.freechild.org) from Hart, R.
(1994). *Children's Participation: From Tokenism to Citizenship*. New York: UNICEF.

For Further Thought

1. Using Roger Hart's Ladder of Student Involvement, give examples
    of strategies you might use in order to stand on the top rung of this
    ladder, as often as possible, alongside the children in your life.
2. Think about the ways in which the language we use when talking
    with children conveys or does not convey respect. For example, are
    there ways that we can acknowledge children's accomplishments
    without using phrases such as "you're so big," or "you're so grown
    up," which imply being older is better?
3. Discuss the idea of making spaces for children "as safe as *necessary*
    rather than as safe as *possible*." Give examples of spaces in your envi-
    ronment that can be changed based on this mindset. How would you
    go about making these changes?

CHAPTER 4

Children as Community Protagonists

In celebration of the 10th anniversary of the United Nations Convention on the Rights of the Child, UNICEF Canada and Elections Canada launched a country-wide effort to educate schoolchildren about their rights and provide children an opportunity to vote for the right they deemed most important (Howe & Covell, 2005). Opposition to this effort was strong. Critics warned that if children learned about and discussed their rights, they would believe themselves entitled to say and do whatever they pleased. Adult authority would be undermined, and young people would become undisciplined, irresponsible, and perhaps even dangerous (see also Lansdown, 1996). Opponents further argued that an emphasis on rights would focus children on private concerns at the cost of public spiritedness, and they would grow into apathetic citizens uninterested in civic duty (Howe & Covell, 2005).

Around the same time as the children's election in Canada, several influential social scientists in the United States voiced parallel concerns about the demise of civic life. In outlining the Communitarian movement, for example, Amitai Etzioni (1993, 1996) argued that an overconcern with individual rights came at the expense of commitments to family, friends, and community. As another example, Robert Putnam (1996, 2000) observed that in the latter half of the 20th century, U.S. citizens had become less and less involved in community institutions, preferring to engage in more solitary pursuits (see also Bellah, Madsen, Sullivan, Swidler, & Tipton, 1985).

Although people of all ages and communities worldwide face the challenge of balancing self-interest and community interest, education about human rights does not appear to tip the balance toward self-interest. The results of the election in Canada showed critics' fears to be unfounded. Children did not prioritize their personal freedoms, but affirmed the importance of social connections. Canadian children contended that the most important right for children was the right to grow up within a family. Such results are not unique to Canada. Other countries have held similar elections and found that young people who study children's rights express deep concerns about social connections and civic life. In Mozambique, children voted the right to name, nationality, and family as most important. In Belize and Mexico, children cast the most votes for the right to an education. In Colombia, children chose the right to a safe environment as paramount (Howe & Covell, 2005). When young people become aware of the issues of children's rights, their understanding tends to manifest itself in prosocial concerns about far-reaching issues of fairness, rather than a preoccupation with self-interest. Craig Kielburger (1998) serves as an excellent example of this. He learned about children's rights as a child in Canada and dedicated himself to ending unfair child labor practices across the globe.

The philosopher Bertram Bandman (1999) stated:

> Rights need not be understood primarily as expressions of unrestrained individual liberties, nor do people who favor rights show inadequate concern for the good of others. Rights may instead be interpreted as expressions of human respect, dignity, and maturity. (p. 5; see also Nutbrown, 2001)

In previous chapters of this book, the authors have emphasized self-expression and self-determination as integral to children's rights. We have tried to show why adult society needs to attend to children's voices and ways to achieve this goal. We believe that each community member, regardless of age, has a right (and a responsibility) to express her or his perspective. At the same time, community life depends on the attunement of one's own voice with the voices of others. Each citizen also has a right and responsibility to listen to and honor other people's perspectives. Rights and responsibilities are inextricably linked, and respecting children's rights also means fostering children's respect for the rights of others.

Even young children understand that rights exist within a network of social responsibilities. Children recognize that negotiating multiple perspectives in an effort to honor the needs and wishes of many is a key challenge of communal life. Consider the following pairs of entries in the Boulder Journey School Charter on Children's Rights:

- Children have a right to touch everything, but gently, but not birds because that can scare them very much.
- Children have a right to help other people and even birds with broken wings (so it's okay for people to touch them).
- Children have a right to watch kid TV shows, but not adult shows (because they are boring).
- Children have a right to watch adult TV shows if Mom or Dad says 'okay,' like Enterprise or Survivor.

In reading these entries, one can almost hear the give-and-take that occurred in the exchanges of a small group of children dedicated to articulating their ideas about rights. The constructors of the Boulder Journey School Charter on Children's Rights sought to build knowledge together, and as a result their understanding of rights became complex and nuanced. Through their efforts to attend to varying perspectives, they uncovered and sought to resolve numerous challenges inherent in the balancing of rights and responsibilities.

This chapter explores how children understand the rights and responsibilities essential to community life, and how adults can promote children's understanding. We explore how to support children as *protagonists* in communities, that is, actors, agents, and co-constructors of civic life.

THE SOCIAL CONTEXT OF CHILDREN'S COMMUNAL RESPONSIBILITIES: PARENTS, TEACHERS, AND PEERS

Human development professor Eliot Turiel (2002) noted that in all cultures and social relationships, people must strike a balance between individualism and collectivism. Furthermore, he noted that those with more authority and power have greater freedom to choose independence and autonomy. Within families and schools, adults have greater opportunities for autonomy, while children's embeddedness in the social contexts of family and school means that their ability to survive and thrive depends a great deal on their sensitivity to those around them.

A view of children as socially attuned contrasts with prevailing views of children as self-centered. Although research in child development historically has questioned the ability of infants and young children to experience empathy, in the 1980s numerous scholars argued that emotional responsiveness to the social world begins at an early age (e.g., Eisenberg 1982, 1986, 1992; Hoffman, 1982, 2000). Indeed, recent research shows that children as young as 18 months sympathize with people who find themselves in negative situations, even if those people offer no affective clues about their distress (Vaish, Carpenter, & Tomasello, 2009). Psychologist William Damon (1988) noted, "Newborns have the capacity for some purely affective empathic responses. These early feelings become the emotional cornerstone of prosocial behaviour" (p. 15). As children mature, they add to this emotional cornerstone of empathic responsiveness an increasing capacity to recognize the emotions of others and to understand how they can affect others' emotions. This growing social sensitivity occurs alongside children's efforts to understand and articulate their own emotions and ideas. The assertions of these child development scholars are supported by many educators, including teachers at Boulder Journey School, who encounter numerous and compelling examples of young children's empathy (e.g., Quann & Wein, 2006).

The family is the first context in which children learn the rules of social participation and are obligated to abide by those rules (Damon, 1988). Families operate as systems, and members must negotiate ever-changing relationships as family resources and responsibilities are apportioned in a way that allows all members to flourish.

Although family life matters a great deal, schools offer unique opportunities for children to develop their understanding of communal life. Traditionally, schools have focused on individual achievement, but they are inherently social organizations. The educational philosopher Loris Malaguzzi held that school is at its core a system of relationships (Edwards, 1995). Relationships are not always at the forefront of educators' thinking about the purpose of schooling, but schools are, nonetheless, communities in which teachers and children come together to

FIGURE 4.1. Children recognize the emotions of others and understand how they can affect others' emotions. © Boulder Journey School, 2010.

learn. They are public entities invested in helping children become contributors to the common good. The public, prosocial nature of schools led John Dewey (1909) to encourage educators to "take the child as a member of society in the broadest sense and demand for and from the schools whatever is necessary to enable the child intelligently to recognize all his social relationships" (cited in Gans, 1952, p. 137). When attention to social responsibilities is overt and considered, schools can provide "the necessary balance so that individual success can be set within the context of public good and individualism set within a context of a local and global community" (Berman, 1997, p. 203).

Given the importance of schools to children's sense of communal responsibility, it is notable that educational institutions in the United States tend to focus on young people as *future* citizens. Adults emphasize the importance of preparing children to participate in a democracy as adults, rather than ensuring that they are part of democracies as children. For example, some public systems in the United States, such as the courts, are mandated to consider children's ideas in matters that concern them. There is, however, no similar mandate that educational systems consider the views of children (Lansdown, 1994).

Despite the lack of legal mandate, children's involvement in decisions within educational systems is crucial to their well-being and development. Alfie Kohn, the author of numerous books on children and education, stated that one of the most important distinctions in education is the distinction between teachers telling students what is and isn't permitted, and teachers bringing students together to consider how they can live and learn as a community. "It is the difference between being prepared to spend a lifetime doing what one is told and being prepared to take an active role in democratic society" (cited in S. Hart & Hodson, 2004, p. 30). The authors agree that participation in democratic learning communities fosters the future goal of responsible citizenship *and also* serves the current goal of respecting children's rights as citizens in the present.

Although parents, teachers, and other adults play an important role in promoting children's sense of themselves as community protagonists, a role this chapter explores, it is also important to acknowledge that adults may overestimate our significance to children's communal life. In a study of parent and child views of quality in childcare, researchers found that parents tend to evaluate settings based largely on their assessments of staff competence. Children, on the other hand, deemed other children the most important determinant of quality (Langsted, 1994). Of secondary importance to children were the setting's activities, toys, and staff, all of which they weighted as equally important. As another example of the paramount importance of community for children, remember the story told in Chapter 1 of a teacher who thought children might appreciate the opportunity to eat lunch when they were hungry, rather than at a time prescribed by adults. They did not. Children understood that if everyone ate lunch on their own schedule, they would eat alone. "It is important to eat with friends and it's sad without."

Scholars who emphasize the importance of peers over adults may encounter considerable resistance to this notion. In 1998, the author Judith Harris caused an enormous stir in the psychological community by suggesting that peers affect child development more than parents. Expanding on the work of the ethnologist Irenaus Eibl-Eibesfeldt, Harris (1998) noted that it does indeed take a village to raise a child.

> But the reason it takes a village is not because it takes a quorum of adults to nudge erring youngsters back onto the path of righteousness. It takes a village because in a village there are always enough kids to form a playgroup. 'It is in such play groups that children are really raised.' (p. 161)

Judith Harris was not the first scholar to note the significance of peers. Many great thinkers have argued that young people learn about interacting within communities from other young people. The anthropologist Margaret Mead stated that one cannot talk of *the* child but only of children as social beings constantly interacting and learning good and bad from one another, reinventing culture together (Moore, 1997). Jean Piaget (1932) held that morality develops from peer interactions, not as a result of mandates from adult authorities. More recently, William Damon (1988) argued that in their relationships with adults, children learn about

> social order, prescribed social rules, and the moral rationales behind them. In their relationships with peers, however, children learn strategies for interacting,

such as reciprocity and negotiation. Once the child learns to use these procedures, the child will become able to work out moral rules democratically with others all through life. (p. 86)

Because children's relationships with other children are so crucial, adults gain great power from their ability to affect peer interactions. In one study, 410 undergraduate students with majors in education and psychology described their best and worst memories of school. The researcher expected best memories to be associated with successes at school, and they were. The worst memories, however, did not reflect encounters with school failure, as anticipated. Worst memories consisted of experiences with humiliation. One respondent remembered having tape placed over her mouth as punishment for talking out of turn in class. Others recalled having papers torn up or being hit in front of classmates (Rothenberg, 1994). The use of dunce caps may have lost favor in modern schools, but as in the days of old, much of the "teacher's power resides in her ability to put individual children in the spotlight, to make them the focus of their peers' attention. She can, if she is so inclined, hold up a child to public ridicule or public envy" (Harris, 1998, p. 241).

If a teacher has the power to influence social relationships within the classroom, it would stand to reason that this power could be used to facilitate, as well as damage, the sense of community among peers. The notion that a key role for teachers is to facilitate peer relationships lies at the heart of the concept of *supportive social learning*, a means of creating caring classroom communities developed at Boulder Journey School (Hall & Rudkin, 2003). Supportive social learning has four defining features:

- Community members value and seek to include everyone in creating a sense of community;
- The nurturing of relationships among community members takes precedence over other agendas;
- Children are seen as capable of overcoming problems and succeeding socially as individuals and as a group;
- The teacher enters all classroom interactions with a questioning posture and commitment to conversation.

THE ROLE OF ADULTS IN SUPPORTING CHILDREN AS COMMUNITY PROTAGONISTS: STEPPING IN AND STEPPING OUT

One of the most common misconceptions about supportive social learning is that it corresponds with permissive teaching. The notion of permissive teaching draws heavily on Diana Baumrind's (1966, 1967) classic work on parenting styles. Baumrind identified two extremes of parenting, authoritarian and permissive parenting (she subsequently divided the permissive style into two separate styles:

permissive-indulgent and permissive-neglectful), and a third style, authoritative parenting, which combines elements of both. Authoritarian parents judge and control their children according to a strict standard of proper behavior. They value obedience rather than collaboration, and rely on punishment and force to compel children toward proper conduct. Authoritarian parents restrict children's autonomy while expecting them to assume many responsibilities. Permissive parents, on the other hand, make few demands for responsibility or for orderly conduct. They foster children's autonomy as much as possible, allowing them to self-regulate activities. Permissive parents are nonpunitive and noncontrolling. The third parenting style, authoritative parenting, combines elements of the other two styles. Authoritative parents honor children's voices. They involve children in decision making, but also make their own viewpoints known as they guide children. Baumrind found that the authoritative style resulted in the best outcomes. Children of authoritative parents were both self-assertive *and* socially skilled.

Teachers invested in the defining features of supportive social learning have found the authoritative style instructive (e.g., Fraser & Gestwicki, 2001). Although authoritative adults, as described by Baumrind, are highly directive and retain an emphasis on adult authority, they resemble adherents of supportive social learning in their effort to achieve a balance between child and adult perspectives, and also between individual autonomy and social responsibility.

One reason for the confusion between supportive social learning and permissive teaching is that the classrooms of teachers who use supportive social learning may resemble classrooms of permissive teachers. Children may, for example, seem quite loud as they excitedly move about the classroom individually or in small groups. The teacher's presence is certainly less evident than the presence of more authoritarian teachers who value order and who direct classroom activities, but teachers in socially supportive classrooms are most definitely present. They may not be the center of classroom attention, but they are listening carefully, documenting events in order to help children extend their work together, and ready to step in when children desire assistance.

Respecting children's rights and autonomy does not mean leaving them to act and decide on their own. It means being available as a support and guide when needed and stepping back to allow children to engage in their own process when possible. As the young crafters of the Boulder Journey School Charter on Children's Rights put it:

- Children have a right to tell parents and teachers to help them if they have a big problem.
- Children have a right to solve their own problems whenever they can.

Adult *involvement* in the lives of children is not synonymous with adult *infringement*. In a children's rights project that occurred in Norway (Kjørholt, 2003), the adults were so concerned about curtailing children's autonomy, they refused to lend their expertise. This created a paradox. The goal of this empowerment project was to provide children with support "on their own terms."

> However, as it turned out, the adults laid down these terms by virtually 'forcing' the children to decide for themselves, in the process prohibiting them from using adults as important resources of expertise and skill, even when they [the children] wished to do so. (p. 201)

As described in Chapter 3, adults have more experience than children and have useful wisdom to impart. Adults might, for example, have expertise to offer with regard to personal hygiene and timekeeping. Consider these entries from the Boulder Journey School Charter on Children's Rights:

- Children have a right to brush their own teeth (and parents have a right to check their teeth when the children are done brushing).
- Children have a right to know what time it is, and how many minutes they have to wait for something (their turn), and the time it will be when it's finally their turn.

An image of children as competent leads adults to expect children to accomplish much on their own. At the same time, children's honest assessment of their limitations may constitute another sign of competence. Adults, too, seek expert help. Calling in a plumber to complete a home renovation, for example, may not signal incompetence, but rather demonstrate good sense.

A project that began at Boulder Journey School in 2002 illustrates how adults can lend expertise while respecting children's rights and responsibilities. A classroom of 4-year-olds decided to construct "Saturn 5: The Largest Rocket Ship Ever Built" (Maher & Sieminski, 2006). Although the children had experience designing projects and using tools, they quickly realized that their vision outstripped their capabilities. Children knew they did not have the physical strength to lift large pieces of wood or the knowledge of carpentry required to make the rocket sturdy. The children wrote a letter to their parents:

Dear Moms and Dads,
We would like your help. We are making Saturn 5—the Largest Rocket Ever Built. Please do the hard jobs like nailing the floors together and attaching the wood pieces together. We want the rocket ship to be tall and pointy. We want to have lots of space in Saturn 5. We want to have enough space for more people to come in it. We want the shape of the rocket ship to be tall and pointy. We will make the engine and the rocket boosters.
Please come to school on Wednesday, October 2 at 6:00 p.m. If one of you stays at home with me then the other one can come. Or, maybe you can hire a babysitter so that you can both come to school.

>   We are excited to come to school the next morning and see what you
>   built for us.
>   Thank you for helping us!

The children's parents eagerly offered their assistance. They drew sketches based on the children's blueprints and generated a list of necessary materials, which they collectively gathered and purchased. On October 2, 11 parents met in the classroom and built the frame of the rocket out of wood. They remained at school until late into the night, sharing in their children's excitement about this project. The construction of Saturn 5 (Figure 4.2) engulfed the entire classroom community.

The assistance the 4-year-olds needed in constructing Saturn 5 was specific to the capabilities the children possessed at that point in time. The parents would have been called upon in a different way if the children were 2 years old or if they were 12 years old. Honoring children's rights and responsibilities means negotiating an interdependence that continually shifts based on many different aspects of a situation. These aspects include what the United Nations Convention on the Rights of the Child referred to as the "evolving capacities" of the children (and, perhaps, of the adults, too!).

Children's rights activist Anne Smith (2002) noted, "Children's development and their capacity to participate with an increasing degree of responsibility, is initially highly dependent on the supportiveness of the social and cultural context" (p. 85). As children gain skills and confidence, however, the involvement of the social context may become less necessary. The United Nations Convention on the Rights of the Child advised that dialogue is key to this process so that "the child will gain an understanding of why particular options are followed, or why decisions are taken that might differ from the one he or she favored" (UNICEF, n. d.).

Adults committed to nurturing children as community protagonists help children exercise their rights and assume responsibilities to the greatest extent possible. They also ensure that what is possible, continually expands. The Russian psychologist Lev Vygotsky (1978) introduced the notion of the zone of proximal development—the difference between the capabilities children demonstrate on their own and what they demonstrate with the scaffolding of others. At Boulder Journey School, teachers attempt to involve children in community processes at the outer limits of their zones of proximal development in the belief that children are more capable community protagonists than common knowledge leads us to expect. They also believe that children's capacity to act in socially responsible ways comes from opportunities to rise to social challenges. In other words, "Children become competent by first being treated as if they are competent" (Alderson, 1994, p. 56).

VALUING CONFLICT

Research suggests that when children have opportunities to exercise their rights, use their voices, and make choices, the number of disagreements with adults de-

FIGURE 4.2. Saturn 5: The largest rocket ever built. © Boulder Journey School, 2010.

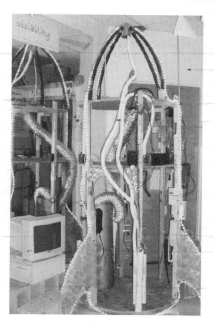

creases, but disagreements with other children increase (Langsted, 1994). This outcome may seem problematic. Even in traditional classrooms, disagreements among children, especially young children, are commonplace. One study found that conflicts among toddlers occur every 5 minutes (Bayer, Whaley & May, 1995). Furthermore, this number does not reflect the arguments of just a few children who cannot get along. In a 10-week study of 53 preschoolers, only one child was *not* observed in a quarrel (Laursen & Hartup, 1989). Conflicts around sharing are particularly common, arising from the moment children first interact with one another (Damon, 1988) and continuing, in some fashion, throughout life.

The ubiquitous nature of social conflicts suggests that they are somehow necessary. Perhaps they are even desirable. The work of adults committed to promoting children as community protagonists is greatly enhanced if adults can value disagreement. Piaget and his followers highlighted the importance of *cognitive* disequilibrium to growth, but it may be that development, especially moral development, advances primarily from *social* disequilibrium (Haan, 1985).

Adults' discomfort with children's conflict may result from assumptions about disagreements that adults make but children do not share. As described in Chapter 3, children tend not to be as attached to their own ideas as adults are, and as a result may disagree more easily. This is illustrated by the young child who advised, "Not everybody thinks the same. If somebody thinks like you, she's a nuisance" (Reggio Children, 1995, p. 48).

Adults tend to see crises where children see mere disagreements. Disagreements consist of resistance toward others without strong sadness or anger, while crises are resistance to others accompanied by powerful emotions (see Singer & Hannikainen, 2002, for more on this distinction). The duration of children's arguments supports the view that children's arguments tend to be mere disagreements. Children's arguments tend to be short-lived. In a classic study of 200 quarrels among children, only 13 endured for more than 1 minute (Dawe, 1934). More recent research suggests that most disagreements among preschoolers are resolved within 10 seconds (Laursen & Hartup, 1989). Moreover, after the conflict ends, children usually resume their play together with no residual bad feelings (Dawe, 1934; Laursen & Hartup, 1989). Children seem to understand, better than adults, the necessity of grabbing, stomping, or even hitting and biting as means of self-expression for young people with limited words and a lack of experience in social interaction. Young children in conflict may argue, and even physically hurt one another, without the acerbity adults would feel when interacting in a similar fashion (McKay, 1990). Thus, adults watching conflicts may experience much more discomfort than the toddlers directly involved in the conflict (Da Ros & Kovach, 1998).

Adults in the United States tend to see conflict as crises or potential crises. Adults also tend to view conflicts as manifestations of individual children's aggression, rather than an inevitable part of social interaction (Shantz, 1987). In Japanese classrooms, conflict is seen as a class-level rather than an individual-level concern (Lewis, 1996). As another manifestation of the individual focus of U.S. culture, natives of this country usually subscribe to the notion that when people think about events differently, one person's viewpoint is better than the other's. In other cultures such as Japanese, Mandenko, and Navajo, differences are seen instead as valuable opportunities for a richer understanding of a situation (Maruyama, 1983).

The prevalent views about conflict in U.S. culture lead adults to see children's disagreements as disrupting, rather than promoting, social connections. Disagreements may be, however, a manifestation of caring and an opportunity for greater understanding. Research suggests that preschoolers more frequently quarrel with friends as compared with nonfriends (Hartup & Laursen, 1991; Hartup, Laursen, Stewart, & Eastenson, 1988). This makes sense, of course, as friends spend much more time interacting, feel freer to express themselves openly, and care about the outcome of their disagreements.

In summary, adults in the United States tend to see children's conflicts as crises, as a sign of individual aggression, and as threatening to the social order. Such notions about conflict make adults uncomfortable when children disagree. In addition, adults may question children's ability to resolve conflicts effectively and may feel acutely responsible for ensuring children's safety and well-being. These factors taken together compel adults to intervene quickly and forcefully when conflicts among children occur.

Adults often attempt to prevent arguments among children as much as possible and resolve those that occur with great haste (Da Ros & Kovach, 1998; Singer & Hannikainen, 2002). The tendency to overregulate conflicts and hurry to peaceful resolution lead adults to judge situations, make pronouncements (e.g., "That's not nice"), assign blame, and devise consequences. Some research finds that adults decide on the solution to children's conflicts without the input of children 91% of the time (Killen & Turiel, 1994). It may be, however, preferable for adults to resist rushing to solutions, and instead make space for children to express their feelings and viewpoints and to resolve problems themselves to the greatest extent possible. First, children will feel respected, trusted, appreciated, and in control (because they are!). Second, children will be able to devise resolutions that are meaningful and satisfying.

When my younger son was 4, his battery-powered car turned out to be of great interest to a young guest who delighted in riding it around the circle outside our home over and over. At some point, my son decided it was his turn to ride, and I heard him objecting quite vociferously to his friend's unwillingness to relinquish the car. I approached the twosome to find out what was happening. The friend suggested that my son could ride as the passenger, but this did not satisfy the desire to take a turn behind the wheel. I asked my son how many times he had gotten to drive around the circle and he said he had driven around two times. I asked his friend if this sounded right, and he agreed. I asked my son's friend how many times he had gone around. He claimed to have driven around the circle about 100 times. My adult mind quickly calculated that an equitable solution might involve 98 additional revolutions for my son, but this was not the solution either of them devised. My son wanted only one more turn, which his friend was happy to allow. Our guest then resumed his driving as my son happily engaged in other activities.

Children's ideas about conflict resolution sometimes include the establishment of rules. When a conflict occurs in traditional classrooms, the teachers make a rule and inform the children. In more participatory classrooms, teachers and children consider the problem together. If children actively participate in creating the rules, they have a better understanding and reasoning of why the boundaries are necessary (e.g., Solomon, Watson, & Battistich, 2001). As a result, the teacher need not assume the role of enforcer. Instead, the children remind one another of their agreed-upon standards of behavior.

The Saturn 5 project, introduced earlier in the chapter, provoked considerable interest in space and space travel, and led to the notion that a moon buggy was essential to the project. A parent who worked as an engineer at Ball Aerospace (a company that provides technological support for national policymakers, the U.S. military, and NASA) agreed to construct the shell of a moon buggy with and for the children. When the moon buggy shell arrived at school, all other plans for the day were put on hold to make room for the children's excitement. The children who had requested the buggy went to the school's studio and chose materials to enhance the moon buggy. They selected a speaker to use as a headlight, a steering wheel to drive the buggy, a big empty water jug to serve as an air tank, a red light to use as a brake light, and a keyboard for a control panel.

News of the moon buggy quickly spread throughout the school. Everyone wanted to see it, touch it, and play on it. Within hours, the moon buggy had lost some of the parts the children had added. The children who had helped to bring the moon buggy to the school determined that they needed to establish rules about how to use the moon buggy. A small group of children discussed possible rules and eventually created a list that they distributed and reviewed with all of the children and teachers in the school. The children's rules indicated that they were concerned with the care of their treasured moon buggy:

- Please do not draw on the moon buggy.
- Please do not throw stuff at it.
- Please sit in the seats . . . not on the back or the front of the buggy.
- Please do not pull on it.
- Don't jump on it.
- Don't spit at it.

Their list of rules also suggested that they wanted to protect the safety of the children using the moon buggy:

- No climbing on the moon buggy . . . only sitting on it.

The children considered how the addition of a moon buggy in the hallway might affect the school community, especially the nearby classrooms:

- Remember to use inside voices.

And last, the children wanted everyone interested in the moon buggy to enjoy themselves:

- Two friends can sit on the moon buggy. If you are not sitting on the moon buggy and want to play, you can look around at the things in space, play at the rocket ship or the space station, read books about space, or look for moon rocks.

Children understand that "sharing is often the price of admission to social activity" (Damon, 1988; p. 32), and so are motivated to resolve conflicts without adult intervention. Although adult expertise can smooth the negotiation process, adult pronouncements will not likely have the desired effect of resolving conflicts and instilling moral values. In order to develop social skills, children need to make the process their own. Research into children's ideas about sharing illustrates this point well. When children were asked to justify their prosocial acts, they rarely implicated adults. They did not share because teachers or parents told them that they needed to or that it was the right thing to do, but because of their *own* convictions. Children do not strive to be fair in an effort to obey adult authority, but rather for moral, empathic, or pragmatic reasons of their own (Damon, 1988).

CHILDREN AS PROTAGONISTS IN GLOBAL (AS WELL AS LOCAL) COMMUNITIES

Children learn and grow through their relationships with other children, becoming protagonists of the communities in which they reside and communities beyond their own homes and schools. Educator Carolyn Edwards (1995) proposed that the classroom exists nested within ever-larger surrounding communities. Early friendships "represent one way in which children enter and become active in a wider community, outside the family, co-constructing with children their own cultural forms . . . and increasing their sphere of social influence" (Moss & Petrie, 2002, p. 104).

Adults mediate young children's involvement in the wider community; thus, access to information and children's ability to take action depend on the adults'

**FIGURE 4.3. Creating a moon buggy was essential to the Saturn 5 project. ©
Boulder Journey School, 2010.**

willingness to facilitate children's participation. Sometimes adults seek to prevent children's contact with the larger world. The popular image of the child as an "innocent," living in a golden age of carefree play and sunshine, necessitates a protected space separate from the sometimes harsh, "real" world of adults. Sentimentalized visions of childhood, however, deny the reality of children's citizenship. Gunilla Dahlberg and her colleagues (1999) stated, "If we hide children away from a world of which they are already a part, then we not only deceive ourselves, but do not take children seriously and respect them" (p. 45).

Waldorf

At Boulder Journey School, teachers continually find that children know about and are concerned with world events. As one example, on August 29, 2005, one of the deadliest hurricanes in history occurred—Hurricane Katrina. Even though the hurricane occurred hundreds of miles away from Colorado, many of the 3- and 4-year-old children worked together to understand and cope with this event. Devin expressed his appreciation for the availability of information:

> When there is a hurricane, people get sick and have to go to a hospital, and then they put it on TV, and then they show people in Colorado what's happening, because they're not bad people and they're good guys, and good guys tell people.

The children worked to make meaning of this cataclysmic event through their *words*, such as this explanation by Annie:

FIGURE 4.4. Children were concerned with the care of their treasured moon buggy. © Boulder Journey School, 2010.

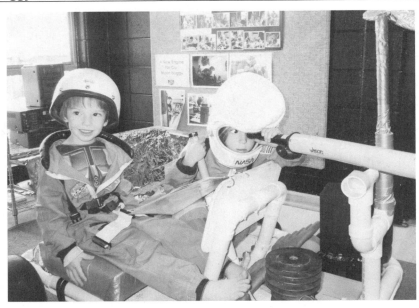

A hurricane is when a lot of water vaporates from the ocean and goes up into the air, and it makes big clouds, and it has a hurricane. It vaporates into the air and pushes the waves higher. Vaporates means it comes from the ocean and it really goes into the air and the water vaporates and makes a cloud.

The children also used *drawing and painting* as a way of making sense of this cataclysmic event, as seen in the watercolor (Figure 4.5) by *Jackson:* "This is the ocean that the hurricane flies over. It's very angry." And, the children sought meaning in this catastrophe through their play. Figure 4.6 depicts the shelter for hurricane survivors that children constructed on the playground climber.

The children not only wanted to make sense of this important world event, but also wanted to assist the people affected by the hurricane. One conversation among several children began when Jackson asked, "Can we talk about how to help them?"

> *Annie:* We should make another sale of just money, so they can have money to buy more stuff and move houses and suck the water off the land.
>
> *Jackson:* We might build them a house for them to live in.
>
> *Annie:* But look at when they don't have any houses, and they have to live with no roofs or houses, just furniture.
>
> *Alex:* We could find some seashells that are really pretty and smell for them.

Eli: 150 stoplights broke down.

Alex: You could maybe dive in to get them.

Jackson: If we had a life jacket on.

Alex: If we had an airplane we could get them.

Jackson: And we could put the ladder down for them to climb up.

Alex: And they could fly here.

Jackson: But their airport is still far away.

Alex: Maybe we could fly a jet, because it's faster.

Annie: We should get them more food.

Jackson: We could get the fastest plane . . . but how are we going to do all this?

Annie: We should call them and tell the fastest airplanes to get them here fast.

Jackson: We can write them a note to tell them they should fly on an airplane . . . or write them one letter to see what they need at school . . .

Annie: . . . and one letter to see what they need at home.

Alex: Maybe we could talk to them.

Jackson: On the phone you mean?

Alex: Yeah, on the phone to see what they need.

Jackson: We know we can't fly a plane there, because it's a really long way.

Annie: They need paintbrushes . . . I have some sand in my shed.

Alex: I wanted to bring all my money from my piggy bank to the hurricane.

Children are concerned about world events and have creative ideas about what should be done. When faced with the enormous catastrophe of Hurricane Katrina, the children wished to take enormous actions. They were not afraid to think big, but also developed together a sense of what they realistically could do. They expressed empathy for those affected by the hurricane, and although they first proposed actions that seemed compelling to them, they soon realized the importance of finding out what sort of assistance those affected by the hurricane would find most helpful. With the help of their teachers, the children in this classroom began correspondences with schoolchildren in New Orleans and sent them needed materials.

CONCLUSION

Adults intent on promoting children as community protagonists carefully listen to children and communicate that what children say and do matters. We include children in discussions about important issues and do not constrain their participation to trivial concerns. Perhaps more significant, our goal is not to bring children into

FIGURE 4.5. A 4-year-old child's watercolor of Hurricane Katrina. © Boulder Journey School, 2010.

adult decision-making processes, but to engage with children in dialogue about *their* processes in order to make these processes more visible to us and to them. To support children in *their* processes requires listening to their many languages (see Chapter 1). It may mean offering words or gestures or other materials to support the expression of their thoughts, feelings, and opinions. During the United Nations Convention on the Rights of the Child, a Children's Forum was held with seven children to discuss children's participation. These children noted that other important roles for adults include providing children with the information needed to make decisions, allowing children the space and time to make decisions, and also allowing mistakes and not responding to missteps by absolving children of responsibility. They concluded, "We need adults to guide us towards making good decisions, but we also need you to let us practice making the wrong decisions as well" (cited in Smith, Gollop, Marshall, & Nairn, 2000, p. 17).

For Further Thought

1. Recall a tragedy that occurred during your childhood. This could be a salient event in your family, community, the nation, or the world. Describe what happened and how you felt. What information did you have about this event and how did you gain this information? What did adults and/or other children do to help you to understand and/or cope with this event? What do you wish had happened that didn't?

2. Discuss the prevailing views on disagreement in our culture and in your own life. Do you think these views are problematic? If so, what strategies might potentially alter them?

FIGURE 4.6. Children constructed a shelter for Hurricane Katrina survivors on the playground climber. © Boulder Journey School, 2010.

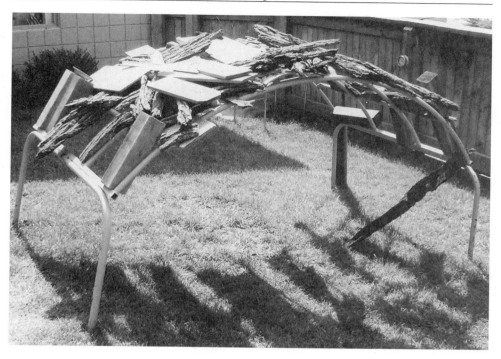

3. Describe several things that children can do that adults cannot.

4. Invite a group of children to represent their perspectives on children's responsibilities using several different languages, in addition to conversation, such as drawing, photography, poetry, or painting. Note that you may need to find creative ways of asking about "children's responsibilities" in order to receive meaningful answers.

CHAPTER 5

Children's Exploration of Rights Through the Construction of a Hamster City

In the fall of 2004, several children in a 4-year-old classroom at Boulder Journey School developed an interest in building a track for the classroom's pet hamster. Their teacher, Elizabeth Clarkson (2004), decided to tape-record, photograph, and videotape the children's work, not suspecting at the time the richness this project would assume. When the authors encouraged Boulder Journey School teachers to research the issue of children's rights from children's perspectives, Elizabeth wondered if the children's interest in freeing the hamster signified a broader interest in rights. An ever-widening circle of adults has been struck by the depth of the children's thinking about the rights of their hamster, and by their care in creating a world in which these rights were respected. In order to set the stage for considering this study of rights, let us first tell the story of Crystal the hamster, and of the children, teachers, and family members who worked together to build her a city.

A CITY FOR CRYSTAL

In the fall of 2004, Crystal the hamster lived in a small cage in a classroom of 4-year-olds at Boulder Journey School. The only "freedom" she experienced was propelling a plastic exercise ball over a black track that assembled into a loop.

One September morning, two boys began experimenting with the track. They built and rebuilt it over several days and noticed that if they did not put the track together "correctly," the ball rolled off the track and onto the floor. At first the children found the departure from the track exciting, but they soon agreed that it was not safe for Crystal's ball to roll loose in the classroom.

Throughout September, children designed pathways using different materials to block the ends of the tracks so the ball could not roll freely. The designs became increasingly elaborate. They used wooden blocks, Legos, baskets, rocks, and small gems to create bridges, tunnels, and decorations, while always requiring that the structures be "safe for Crystal." Occasionally, comments from someone inspired new ideas, such as one child's assertion that "Crystal would like to be in the city!"

The children began to draw their plans for cities. They sketched squiggly lines and free-form shapes, and used the sketches to explain their ideas to friends. Their cities often featured vigilant flying dinosaurs perched on the buildings, ready to protect Crystal in her ball.

Although the children's designs became more elaborate, they had only a limited number of track pieces. Thus, their block cities remained disconnected from the short expanse of black tracks on which Crystal moved. One day some of the children made an important discovery: The blocks could serve as walls for the exercise ball! If they built walls of blocks, Crystal could roll off the black track onto the floor while remaining on a predetermined and safe course. Moreover, the "track" could be made much longer, and Crystal could propel her ball throughout the entire hamster city.

On November 9, after several days of building and revising the tracks, which now included walls made of blocks, a conversation occurred that changed the course of the project. A boy named Andy proposed, "Guys! Let's build a whole city again! It's gonna be the whole world, right Evan?" The boys worked for 15 minutes, adding blocks and moving them from place to place. Then Ben noted, "This is for Crystal to walk right through. It's the secret passageway." Everyone stopped working and looked at Ben. Andy repeated Ben's radical idea, "Walk?" "Yes," Ben confirmed, "Crystal wants to walk some and drive some." After a pause, Evan validated Ben's suggestion, exclaiming, "She likes to do both in the city!"

Until that day, all of Crystal's time out of her small cage was spent "driving" her exercise ball. Now the children realized they could free Crystal from her ball and allow her to walk safely on her own. The electricity in the air was palpable and the children's thinking exploded. Everyone talked and moved excitedly, conferring about the best height for the walls and sharing concerns that Crystal might swallow the small decorations. Twenty minutes later, the children had made their revisions and, for the first time, the little hamster walked freely inside her city. Teachers gathered in case the need arose to scoop Crystal up, but she walked without incident. It was a great day!

On November 19, a second pivotal meeting occurred. Elizabeth brought four boys and the hamster to a quiet room where the boys could observe Crystal and talk together. The children watched Crystal and conversed for an hour. At this point, the conversation about building a hamster city included a desire to honor Crystal's right to freedom.

> *Cole:* I think she wants out and that's why she nibbles on her cage.
> *Elizabeth*: I've heard two people say that Crystal nibbles on her cage because she wants to get out.
> *Jack:* I think Crystal wants to get out so people will pet her and she will promise not to bite them. . . . If I was a hamster and I was stuck in my cage, I would say, "Please let me out of my cage." I would say that.
> *Ben:* If I was stuck in my cage and someone let me out, I would say

FIGURE 5.1. Crystal the hamster. © Boulder Journey School, 2010.

that I appreciated it and I wouldn't bite anyone anymore. If someone opened the cage and then I won't bite anyone.

Elizabeth: Palmer, if you were stuck in a cage, what would you do?

Palmer: I would say, "Please let me out of this dumb cage."

With this new burst of energy, the teachers wondered if the circle of children involved in the project might expand. A few boys had assumed the role of builders, so the teachers asked several girls if they would like to draw blueprints for Crystal's new city. The girls embraced the opportunity. The drawings accomplished much more than simply providing an opportunity for additional children to work on the project, which had become known as "Hamster Tracks." The drawings also helped resolve the challenge of carrying over ideas from one group to another and from one day to another. In addition, the drawings gave children the chance to dream big and imagine what they could not yet build. Nothing was impossible on paper. Emma describes a drawing (Figure 5.6) she made:

This is Crystal and she's walking on the grass and drinking from the fountain. This is her house with roses and flowers inside her house. She planted them. (Elizabeth: "She did?") We did it for her to smell. This is the ladder to the tree house for her to climb. If she wants to go down, she slides down into the grass. That's connected in case she wants to cross over, because Crystal's so little she might fall (through the slats).

The bottom part is grass and she can eat some of it. . . . This is the window that she looks out of. She's looking at the water. She wants to drink it, so she decides to go outside and see the waves at her house

**FIGURE 5.2. Children designed pathways that became increasingly elaborate. ©
Boulder Journey School, 2010.**

**FIGURE 5.3. The children made an important discovery: The blocks could serve
as walls for the exercise ball! © Boulder Journey School, 2010.**

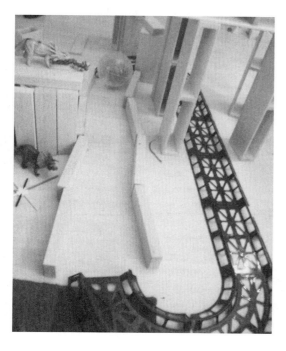

and drink the waves. That's, wait, I'm not done, this part is her bedroom and she's sleeping because it's night. With stairs and rain, and this is the ladder. That's grass.

Throughout the winter, teachers supported the children's efforts to conceive ever-more intricate cities for Crystal. The children became expert designers and builders, and began building the structures they envisioned in their sketches and blueprints. But obstacles remained. The biggest problem was that the structures lasted only a few days. The classroom did not have a secure space to keep the cities, and

**FIGURE 5.4. For the first time, Crystal the hamster walked freely inside her city. ©
Boulder Journey School, 2010.**

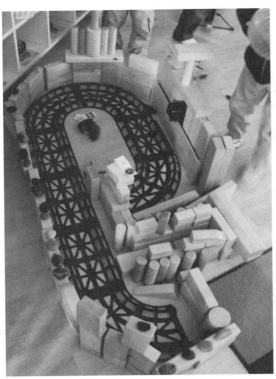

children often needed the blocks and other materials used in the cities' construction for other projects. In January, teachers introduced foam core as a possible building material. It could be cut into endless shapes and attached to other shapes, and was light enough to relocate as needed.

Teachers used an overhead projector to enlarge the photograph of a track children had built from blocks earlier in the year. This image served as the blueprint for a foam core structure.

Two children figured out how to make pieces of the same size by holding one piece of foam core up to another and using a pen to mark the height and length. Children also found a way to construct stairs, solving the dilemma of how Crystal could get from one floor of her multileveled city to the next. The children discovered, by watching Crystal climb over the sides of the stairs, that all walls needed to be at least "two blocks high." From then on, they used "two blocks high" as a standard point of reference.

The children soon reached another impasse. Foam core allowed for flexible designs that could be moved as needed, but it was easily damaged. The children wanted to build a durable city for Crystal. They had visions of a permanent hamster city, but they did not have the technical skill to implement this vision. The children reasoned that parents and other relatives might help build a sturdy city, and the classroom held its first meeting of children and their families on the evening of February 10. Elizabeth and the children shared their work and ideas through slides and photographs, and attendees brainstormed possibilities for a permanent structure. The children's enthusiasm was contagious, and the group decided to meet again the following month to build the hamster city.

The first city-building meeting took place on March 10. The classroom buzzed with excitement as 40 people, adults and children, arrived, tools in hand, to help make the children's ideas a reality. They used plexiglass and wood to replicate the foam core designs. The meeting ended 3 hours later, way past everyone's bedtimes. Crystal now had the beginnings of a permanent city.

[handwritten margin notes: children reasoned !! serious work until family participation]

FIGURE 5.5. Conversation about building a hamster city included a desire to honor Crystal's right to freedom. © Boulder Journey School, 2010.

One advantage of the plexiglass was that it promoted visibility. Children spent the next few weeks observing, documenting, interpreting, and reflecting on Crystal in her new city. Since the beginning of the project, the children had repeatedly tested their ideas by asking, "Is it safe for Crystal?" Now, a second question emerged: "Is Crystal happy?" With Crystal's physical protection ensured, children could concentrate on Crystal's emotional well-being. They talked, for example, about Crystal's need for a family and for hamster playmates.

A month later, in April, the classroom held its second family meeting to elaborate on Crystal's city. The families divided themselves into "work teams" in advance of the meeting, each focusing on a different component of the children's visions: stairs, rope ladders, playground, tree-house platform, and working elevator. The advance organization allowed this meeting to be even more productive than the first meeting despite the involvement of an even larger number of participants—60 children and adults attended. Crystal's city neared completion.

After the second building meeting, the children expressed their desire to share their exciting project with others. They began by inviting members of the school community into their classroom. The children wrote and delivered invitations, and made appointments with other classes. Several children volunteered to be "Hamster Tracks Ambassadors" and eagerly talked about their work with visit-

FIGURE 5.6. A 4-year-old child's drawing of Crystal's city. © Boulder Journey School, 2010.

ing schoolmates. A few children came up with the idea of creating a video in the format of a newscast. They wanted to share the story of Crystal's city widely, "Not just in the school, but outside, in all the houses."

Adults at Boulder Journey School have worked as allies with the children in spreading the word of Crystal and the construction of her city. The school faculty has shared the story in academic papers, at professional conferences around the world, and now in this chapter, the remainder of which highlights insights about rights gleaned from the children's work building a city for Crystal.

THE IMPORTANCE OF MOVEMENT

The children believed that it was unfair to confine Crystal to a small cage, and throughout the project they sought to offer Crystal more and more freedom of movement. Figure 5.11 illustrates the importance children placed on movement.

At first, Crystal's only taste of freedom was propelling her exercise ball around a short circle of track. The children soon decided that Crystal had a right to more freedom, and wanted to make the tracks longer. As Jack stated in October, "It should be longer. From there (couch) . . . to here (behind the futon, which rep-

FIGURE 5.7. An enlarged photograph served as a blueprint for a foam core structure. © Boulder Journey School, 2010.

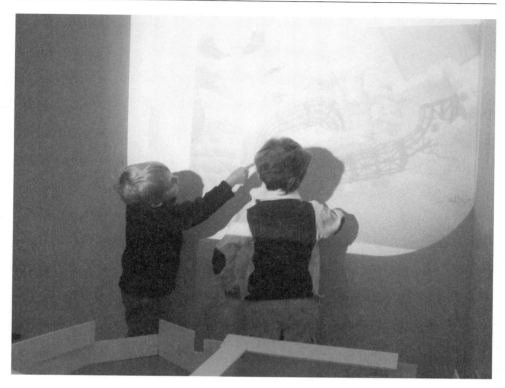

resents a distance of approximately 4 feet). So she could keep going and going and going." When the children ran out of tracks, they came up with the idea of using block walls for the ball to move through. But no matter how long the track, confinement to the ball itself restricted Crystal's freedom. The children noted this in mid-October.

> *Cole:* She keeps going off the track. She wants out. . . . "No," she says, "Get me outta here!"
>
> *Ben:* My idea is to keep her in here (the track area) . . . because she doesn't like it in here (ball). I think she wants to walk through there.

When Elizabeth pointedly asked, "Is it fair for Crystal to stay in her ball?" the response was clear: "No. She's thinking, 'I know I shouldn't have gone in there!'"

Although Ben first mentioned that Crystal could walk outside her ball, it took another month before the revolutionary idea that Crystal could walk caught on with his classmates. In that electric November discussion, Ben reintroduced his notion that Crystal could walk on her own: "This is for Crystal to walk right through. It's the secret passageway."

FIGURE 5.8. Two children figured out how to make foam core pieces of the same size. © Boulder Journey School, 2010.

FIGURE 5.9. Children spent time observing, documenting, interpreting, and reflecting on Crystal in her new city. © Boulder Journey School, 2010.

As adults involved in this project, our appreciation of the link children made between movement and the right to freedom led us to new insights as well. We realized, for example, that the very term used to describe efforts to attain freedom is "movement"—the civil rights *movement*, the women's *movement*, the disability rights *movement*. We also realized that one of the most historically important ways in which disenfranchised groups have asserted their rights is by walking or, more precisely, by marching.

In Chapter 2 we included the lyrics of the African American spiritual/freedom song "All God's Children Got Shoes."

> I got shoes
> You got shoes
> All God's children got shoes
> When I get to heaven gonna put on my shoes
> Gonna walk all over God's Heaven, Heaven, Heaven!

In this song, too, the simple act of walking is transformative. One senses that when the protagonist dons the shoes of freedom for the first time, he or she is changed and no longer feels or looks the same. This may elucidate Jack's initially puzzling exclamation about Crystal: "She'll want to walk around and I want to know what she looks like when she walks."

When the hamster project began, children tied Crystal's movement to the notion of exercise, probably because her first connection to freedom was through her "exercise ball."

FIGURE 5.10. Crystal's city nears completion. © Boulder Journey School, 2010.

FIGURE 5.11. Drawing by a 4-year-old child illustrates the importance of movement. © Boulder Journey School, 2010.

Elizabeth: What does Crystal think about being in her cage?
Cole: Getting out. Because she wants her exercise . . . She's climbing! On the cage. She's going to the top!
Jack: Maybe she's climbing on the top so she can feel like it's life. Yeah!
Elizabeth: What does that mean?
Jack: She's thinking she wants to live . . . to live forever! [November 19]

Although the tie between exercise and freedom appeared most strongly at the start of the project, it emerged in later conversations as well.

She'll love this house! Know why? Because it's bigger than her old house and she'll love the space. She'll walk and walk and walk . . . that's how she'll get her exercise. [January 10]

The children's repeated mention of "exercise" led us to wonder how movement, exercise, and freedom are connected.

For children, movement is crucial to self-expression. Long before they are able to form words children convey their desires through the movement of their bodies—turning, reaching, and pointing. Even after they begin to speak in words, they continue to convey themselves through movement: They express joy through running, jumping, shouting, and spinning; they express anger through pounding, bumping, and stomping, and sometimes hitting and biting. As Maria Montessori (1967) observed, "The need for activity is almost stronger than the need for food" (p. 10). Childhood is characterized by exuberance.

Adults, however, value control over one's body and believe that movement can—and perhaps should—be confined to particular times and places. Adults convey that exuberance is for the playground and the gym—places we go for "exercise" at particular times, such as recess. Adults often make clear to children (and to their parents) that expressive movement does not belong in other locales, such as churches, restaurants, airplane cabins, or even classrooms. Might such restrictions on movement lead children to feel caged?

Although all movement seemed important to the children's desire for Crystal to experience freedom, they repeatedly emphasized upward movement. Mountain climbing served as one symbol of freedom.

> *Jack:* I think she's trying to climb up so she can climb out.
> *Ben:* I got an idea! Maybe she wants to be a mountain climber!
> *Jack:* Yeah! To get out! [November 19]

The symbol of the mountaintop as a place of freedom is clear in Martin Luther King's (1967) most famous speech and also appears in the Charter on Children's Rights (see Chapter 1): "Children have a right to climb mountains, ski on the mountains (when there is snow), and play on the mountains (because the mountains are there for all of us to use)."

The children's designs for Crystal's city featured numerous mechanisms that allowed Crystal to rise up. Crystal's city included mountains and also ramps, stairs, ladders, and even trampolines, rope pulleys, and elevators. Sometimes rewards awaited Crystal at the summit. Here are a few of the numerous mentions of devices that allowed Crystal to move upward:

> This is the ladder. It only has four steps because you can go like, to the haunted house from the bench, it won't be so high. This is the house inside the tree. There's a tunnel from where the bench is to the tree and on the top of the tree are the treasures. [February 7]

> This part is the ladder so she can get up top to all this here (her house and food). [February 22]

> We could make a mountain out of these (shelf liners) and put them here (inside the track area) and she puts her claws in the little holes

FIGURE 5.12. Childhood is characterized by exuberance. © Boulder Journey School, 2010.

and she starts to climb out. Don't worry! I've got plenty of ideas. [March 28]

Almost from the beginning, Crystal's city had more than one tier. In a January conversation, Nate asserted that Crystal's city needed multiple levels. See Figure 5.13 for the picture he drew. Following is the description he provided:

This is the first level and over here is the secret passageway and when she gets out, her house is just there. No one can see her in the secret passageway but we can when she comes out. The slide leads back to the house again. These walls protect Crystal from falling down and this stairs is very high and bumpy. She climbs up the top of the wall and then there's the ladder. She gets to the next level and there's another house. She needs two houses because there are two platforms. The ladder's hard to climb down so she needs two houses so if she needs something she can get it in the house. And then there's a third level that leads to all her food. If she needs to eat, she can climb up there and eat. The water bottle hangs down to drink, upside up. Because it's really hard to drink.

The tie between gaining freedom and upward movement is not unique to children's thinking. Members of oppressed groups often frame the overcoming of oppression as *rising up*. The relationship between upward movement and free-

FIGURE 5.13. A 4-year-old child's drawing illustrates the importance of levels in Crystal's city. © Boulder Journey School, 2010.

dom may have particular relevance for children's rights, however. *Up* clearly matters to children. From the time they are first mobile, children try to get higher by scrambling up staircases, perching on footstools, using pulled-out drawers as steps, pleading to ride on shoulders, or scrambling atop dirt piles where they can become "king of the castle." Things that rise up fascinate children: escalators and elevators, airplanes and helicopters. Part of this fascination may be due to the fact that children are small in an adult-sized world. Participation requires them to be higher so that they can reach sinks, beds, and countertops in ice cream stores. Children also are acutely aware of the link between going up and growing up.

Being confined is part of childhood. Mobility means self-determination, and mobility increases in adulthood. Especially salient to children is the mobility afforded by driving a car. Some children thought this maturity applied to Crystal, as they called Crystal's moving around in her ball "driving." As Cole described:

> I think Crystal's a grown-up because she has her driver's license. She even has a car. If she's a human, she can do whatever she wants when she's old. . . . She can go wherever she wants when she's a grown-up. [March 18]

FIGURE 5.14. A second drawing illustrating the importance of levels in Crystal's city. © Boulder Journey School, 2010.

BALANCING PROTECTION AND PARTICIPATION

One characteristic of a class pet is that it relies on class members for care in a manner that parallels some of the ways children rely on parents. In part, this relates to differences in size and strength. As Nate noted, "Even the kids are big and the hamster is small. She is smaller than us" [February 16].

From the beginning of the hamster project, the children took their role as protectors of the small and vulnerable hamster seriously. Every design innovation needed to pass the test, "Is it safe for Crystal?" Throughout the project, the children took great care in "childproofing" (or in this case hamster-proofing) Crystal's environment. Initially, when Crystal was actually quite safe in her plastic ball on a short track, the children expressed fears for her safety based on fantasy.

> *Nate:* We need dinosaurs to protect them from some of the bad guys. Because some bad guys are just too fast and the dinosaurs have more chances.
> *Alex:* They have 50,000 muscles!
> *Evan:* Crystal doesn't feel safe here because she's scared of the bad guys. We need to protect her! [October 21]

As Crystal gained more and more freedom, the children needed to keep her safe from actual dangers. They removed small decorations that could be swallowed,

FIGURE 5.15. A revised drawing of levels in Crystal's city. © Boulder Journey
   School, 2010.

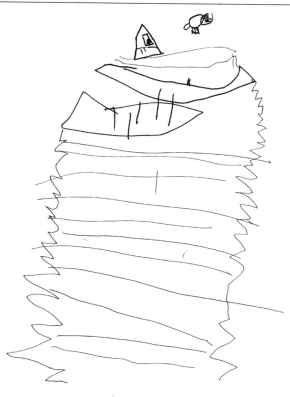

they built walls to keep her from falling, and they provided cushioning in places
where Crystal might slip.

> *Ben:* I'm concerned with the cliff (drop off) because she could fall. . . .
>   She could fall off, she'll need sides.
> *Reilly:* Why don't you put the house on another stand so if she tips
>   over she would land on another piece of wood?
> *Alex:* Maybe something soft?
> *Ben:* Like a landing pad.
> *Emma G.:* Yeah, because Crystal can climb and fall over.
> *Ben:* I would worry so much if she fell. [January 21]

We can use this to put on the stairs so Crystal's feet can stick on them
(slip guard). . . . It needs to be on a platform, see? It needs to have
sides otherwise she will fall right down. [February 7]

Maybe she needs some shade. She might get too hot from the sun. . . .
Maybe she's afraid of heights? Well, we'll just have to try. [February 8]

These quotes make it clear that the children wanted to protect Crystal. But note that they also wanted to give her a chance to try new things, to explore, and even to fall. They were concerned about hamster-promoting as well as hamster-proofing (see Chapter 2 on *childproofing* and *child promoting*). The constant and concerted efforts to ensure Crystal's safety occurred alongside efforts to promote Crystal's autonomy. Even at the beginning of the project, when Crystal was still confined to her ball and the ball was still confined to the track, the children wanted Crystal to have some measure of independence. By forming the track into a loop, they enabled Crystal to propel herself for as long as she liked.

> They need to connect because she wants to go round and round and we don't want to pick her up and put her at the start again. [October 21]

As Crystal gained more and more freedom in her ever-larger and more elaborate city, the idea of two spaces emerged: a large space for adventure, and a smaller place that provided protection. Crystal's cage became not a site of unfair confinement, but a safe haven or home to which she could return after her excursions in the city.

> *Evan:* You know what? I got a great idea. Crystal sleeps in her house during the day because she sleeps and at night she plays. She doesn't like being in her cage because it's not fair but she likes being in her house because she gets to sleep and eat.
> *Jack:* Let's make a rule. Okay, Crystal sleeps in her cage at night and in the daytime she gets to get out. [November 19]

The distinction between inside and outside spaces appeared repeatedly in the children's drawings. Adults involved in this project came to see this as an embodiment of the children's appreciation of the need to balance protection and participation. The children sought to provide opportunities for Crystal's adventure/risk-taking outside and also a safe place inside for her to return and rest. The children created two drawings that show the separate home/indoor and adventure/outdoor spaces (Figure 5.16 & Figure 5.17).

In addition to stairs, ladders, and other mechanisms for moving up, the children's designs included windows, doors, bridges, and passageways. These features often marked the transition from the small, inside, and protected space to the large, outside, and potentially dangerous space.

In the construction of Crystal's city, attention to her right to autonomy came to include Crystal's right to choose between indoor and outdoor spaces via a door.

> Crystal needs a door. Maybe when the door shuts, she can open it. Then she can go in her bedroom. [January 10]

> Then we can make a doorway so she can open and close it herself. [January 21]

Children recognized that even if her cage constituted "home," Crystal would not want to remain forever sheltered and protected. Just as they left the safety of their homes to come to preschool, and would one day soon leave the safety of preschool to attend elementary school, so too would Crystal go out into the unknown world. As Evan, an almost-5-year-old child, observed, "Then Crystal will leave her cage, but she will have to be brave" [November 19].

Although the children designed their cities with two spaces in mind, they set limits on how much freedom Crystal should enjoy—how far "outside" she should go. Children drew pictures of outside spaces that featured flowers and trees. They talked about providing Crystal with a roof to protect her from the rain and shade her from the sun. Crystal's encounters with nature occurred on paper only, however. The children did not want her to leave the classroom. They wanted Crystal to roam free, have adventures, and be happy, but they wanted to provide such opportunities within the confines of her hamster city.

> I'm worried about her getting out of the classroom. She could get squished by a foot! [February 16]

> We were screwdrivering the long pieces in the glass to the wood to make a wall for Crystal because she can bite foam core. But not glass because glass is hard. We had to so Crystal can't get out and she's safe. [March 16]

Although Crystal was taken outside the school on two occasions, teachers initiated both of these excursions. Only one child, Evan, ever suggested Crystal be set free outdoors, and the other children quickly vetoed his idea, enumerating the various dangers she might face.

> *Evan:* Maybe we could release her out to the wild again.
> *Elizabeth:* You think she would want to be released back into the wild?
> *Palmer:* No! She could be eaten by a polar bear! Or a tiger! Or a lion! If she lived in the ocean she could be eaten by a jellyfish and be eaten.
> *Evan:* Yeah. Or she could be eaten by a shark. Or how about a crocodile? Know what? Maybe if she knew how to swim in the water she could just swim, swim, swim. [November 19]

As Tommy foresaw in November: "She will never get out of the city . . . so she'll be safe and not run around the whole school!" Well, at least Crystal would never get out of the city under the watchful eyes of the children. One morning, Elizabeth arrived in the classroom early to get ready for the day. As Elizabeth made her preparations, another teacher checked in on Crystal and called out that she didn't see Crystal in the cage. Elizabeth replied that the hamster liked to hide in the cedar shavings and came over to take a look. She saw that the cage door had been

FIGURE 5.16. A 4-year-old child's drawing illustrates the importance of separate home/indoor and adventure/outdoor spaces in Crystal's city. © Boulder Journey School, 2010.

left open overnight. Crystal was indeed gone. A quick search of the area and panicked visits to neighboring classrooms confirmed that Crystal had disappeared. As the children and their families began to arrive in the classroom, Elizabeth shared the news of Crystal's disappearance, and the children gathered with Elizabeth around the cage and talked about the hamster's great escape. The children were more curious than distraught. They wondered where Crystal wanted to go and what she would do when she got there.

Teachers and children decided to undertake a thorough search of the classroom. They opened cabinet doors, pulled out the furniture, and peered under shelves. The children spoke quietly and moved cautiously so as not to scare or hurt Crystal. When the search proved fruitless, the children sat together on the couch to talk some more. Throughout the year, when children wanted to coax Crystal out of her cedar shavings nest, they spoke in the loving, high-pitched voice one sometimes uses with an infant. They cooed, "Hi there Crystal. . . . Good morning, baby . . . do you want to come out now? You're sooo cute . . . we love you, yes we do." Sitting on the couch now, a boy said in the same loving voice, "Crystal . . . where are you? Please come out now, where are you?"

That's when the little hamster walked out from under the couch and stopped at the children's feet.

Really.

Conversations about Crystal's adventure continued throughout the day and for weeks and months to come. Children discussed where she went on her field trip and what she did. They shared their happiness that after Crystal had found a way to adventure beyond the bounds of her city, she chose to return home.

THE RIGHT TO COMMUNITY— TO CARE AND BE CARED FOR

As the children strove to understand Crystal and what she wanted from life, they became increasingly concerned about her need for community. Children discussed the numerous reasons why family and friends matter—they provide company and comfort, and perhaps most important, playmates.

Initially, the children thought Crystal would like to have people around her.

Crystal wants to be in the city because I think she wants to . . . so we need people. [October 21]

FIGURE 5.17. A second drawing illustrating the importance of separate home/ indoor and adventure/outdoor spaces in Crystal's city. © Boulder Journey School, 2010.

I'm drawing Crystal some people because they are her friends. [November 10]

Crystal would like string that she could play with. And little people to play with. [November 16].

In one of the pivotal conversations in November, when children recognized Crystal's right to freedom, they also recognized her right to family—a *hamster* family. Jack claimed, "Maybe she wants more hamsters. So someone else can be her friend. Yeah."

Children explored possibilities for Crystal to have a family of her own.

Evan: Yeah. Hey, I got an idea! Maybe we can grow some babies for her. She can grow some babies!

Elizabeth: You think Crystal wants to have some babies?

Palmer: Yeah, but, what if Crystal grows babies and she nibbles on them? I think she would.

Jack: Well, I think if Crystal grows babies she will taste them too and that would be bad.

FIGURE 5.18. Drawing by a 4-year-old child depicting Crystal in the tummy of her mother, "Sarah." © Boulder Journey School, 2010.

Palmer: Yeah. Real bad.

Elizabeth: So you don't want Crystal to grow babies?

Jack: Maybe other hamsters. Like big ones that she can't bite.

Palmer: Like daddy hamsters.

Ben: Because she's the mommy!

Elizabeth: You think Crystal is the mommy hamster and she would like a daddy hamster?

Palmer: Yeah and a kid!

Jack: One daddy and two kids.

Ben: One mommy and one daddy and two kids. Crystal is the girl mommy and the boy is the daddy and the kids are a boy and a girl!

The children also talked about Crystal's own parents, and decided that when Crystal came to Boulder Journey School, she had left her mother at the pet store.

Jack: I'll make a carpet for her, so she can feel something soft. Then she'll forget all about her mom and dad. But, she might be scared

in the middle of the night. Well, Crystal doesn't even have a mom.
Evan: But, she had a mom when she was little. But not now. . . .
Jack: When Crystal was at the pet store and you weren't looking, Crystal's mom said, "You're going to go to school with Elizabeth and you might see some teachers and kids." Crystal said, "Oh boy! Now I'm excited!"
Evan: Yeah, she had a mom, but now she's a mom!
Elizabeth: Where are her babies?
Evan: Don't know. Maybe the pet store?
Jack: No, she's not a mom. She's a teenager. That's why it was time to leave the store. [January 18]

As the children explored different ways of providing company for Crystal, the notion of siblings emerged.

Jack: We need a big piece of carpet (at the bottom). . . .
Elizabeth: So Crystal will be safe when she walks down the stairs?
Jack: No, in case she gets a lot of brothers and sisters. . . . We need a whole bunch of them. So she can cuddle with them.
Sophie: And play with them. [February 22]

In November, some children thought their drawings could serve as a replacement for family members. Evan placed a small sticky note in Crystal's cage and declared:

Evan: That's a picture . . . of an old man. It's her grandfather.
Ben: Yeah, and her sister and mother and brother and father.
Elizabeth: Why will Crystal like having pictures of her family in her house?
Jack: Because when she's crying, she'll look at the pictures and it will remind her of her family. [November 9]

By March, however, the children began to recognize limits to playmates for Crystal drawn on paper. They (and their parents) began to form clay companions, and the children talked about three-dimensional playmates.

Reilly: I was thinking of maybe some clay statues for Crystal because I feel special about her. I think she might like to have friends. I was thinking I would get a hamster when I turned 6 years old. I could bring it every day and we could see how they get along with each other and then I'll bring it home every day. [March 7]
Conall: We could make an animal made with paper and I would use glue so it won't break. She could jump on it.
Elizabeth: Crystal would want to jump on the paper animal?
Conall: No, just to play with.

FIGURE 5.19. Drawing by a 4-year-old child depicting Crystal and her twin, in utero, with her parents. © Boulder Journey School, 2010.

Elizabeth: Oh, Crystal wants another animal around?
Conall: She might want it as a "stuffy" (stuffed animal). She might want to sleep with it. [March 30]

Throughout this project, children showed an impressive ability to walk in their hamster's metaphoric shoes. Even in November, a discussion of *why* their hamster sometimes bit led children to conclude that Crystal might feel threatened, asking themselves and one another, "How would you feel if a giant hand came down . . . ?" This evidence counters popular views of young children (also discussed in Chapter 3) as unable to consider the perspectives of others, as promoted in Freud's (1995) work on the "narcissistic infant" and Piaget's (e.g., 1959) discussion of children's "egocentrism" before the age of 8. We found that the children often assumed Crystal's perspective and did so with increasing insight as their relationship with Crystal deepened. For example, their fears for the hamster's safety initially were subsumed into their own fantasy play, which featured powerful dinosaurs. Before long, however, they expressed concern over real dangers in Crystal's environment, such as tall platforms without walls and ingestible decorations. Similarly, the children's desire to provide company for Crystal might have seemed self-centered initially—little people were needed. Later, however, they recognized that despite their best intentions, people were not the ideal company for hamsters. As Emma observed in April, "I think Crystal needs another hamster to push her on the swing! We could do it, but she needs a friend."

CONCLUSION

This chapter describes the work of a small group of children involved in the long-term project of building a city for the class hamster. Although many lessons might be drawn, this conclusion highlights three.

First, this work illustrates that when adults take the time to listen to and amplify the voices of children, the children's deep thinking becomes apparent. Writing the children's words in a different font in this and the previous chapter provides a visual reinforcement of our commitment to amplifying children's voices. When Georgia O'Keefe painted enormous flowers, she confronted viewers with a beauty that few had taken the time to appreciate before. Amplifying voices does not mean simply making children's voices larger or louder, however. Amplifying also involves translating. In writing this chapter, the authors have tried to present the children's words and drawings in a way that (we hope) helps our readers to appreciate the profundity of the children's ideas.

The second lesson is that attending carefully to children's voices requires considerable and continual time and effort. The wisdom of the children featured in this chapter was not always apparent to Elizabeth and her co-teachers during the real time of the project. Many of the children's breathtaking insights emerged as teachers recorded and transcribed the children's conversations, photographed their work, and collected their drawings. They then discussed, revisited, and clarified what they had noticed, first with the children, and later among themselves, with parents and colleagues. This level of attention to children's voices cannot occur all the time. We hope, however, that by sharing the story of Crystal's city, we have reminded our readers, as we have reminded ourselves, that when we make the space to listen more attentively to the children in our lives, they have much to teach us.

The third and perhaps most important lesson pertains to the power of love. The idea in Chapter 3 of adults using the transformative energy of love to overcome children's oppression is an idea that grew from the children's loving work with their hamster. The children sought to care for, respect, and further the life of their hamster without any expectation of reward for themselves. Indeed, they recognized their own limitations in enriching Crystal's life when they realized that

FIGURE 5.20. Families created clay playmates for Crystal. © Boulder Journey
    School, 2010.

some of Crystal's needs could be met only by other hamsters, not by children. The love the children used to guide their work with Crystal serves as a model for how loving adults can both protect and foster the participation of children.

The efforts to build a city for Crystal were clearly transformative for many of the children, and also the adults involved. Why else would 60 people—children, teachers, parents, grandparents and others—show up on an April evening to try and build a hamster-sized elevator? This project changed the children, their families, the teachers, and, hopefully, the rippling effects of this project will touch the readers of this chapter as well.

Is it too far-fetched to believe that in the process Crystal also was changed? When the work with Crystal began, the children handled Crystal with care not only because of her small size, but because she sometimes bit. At some unremarked moment in the course of this project, Crystal stopped biting. And then there was the time Crystal left her cage to explore the world beyond her city. Searches for her proved fruitless, but when the children called her name, the usually reclusive hamster scurried toward them.

Although the children's efforts to build a city for Crystal began as a construction activity, it became an effort to offer Crystal the best possible life. As the school year drew to a close, Elizabeth asked the children to reflect on the hamster city. "Why did we build this?" she asked. Jack spoke for his classmates, "We're just making this so Crystal knows we love her."

For Further Thought

1. Consider the teacher's role in the construction of the hamster city. Identify the moments during the project when important shifts in the children's thinking occur. In what ways does the teacher identify and support these shifts? What else might she have done? How did documentation support this project?

2. Given the link the children made between movement and the right to freedom, and given that children's movement is crucial to their self-expression, discuss strategies for supporting, rather than controlling, children's right to move.

3. Read the story of Crystal with a group of children and ask them to discuss their ideas surrounding protection versus participation. Again, you might need to find creative ways of asking questions about "protection" and "participation" in order to receive meaningful answers.

CHAPTER 6

Children's Places

Crystal's City continued to inspire insights about children's rights long after the young designers moved on to elementary school and Crystal's short life came to an end (although Crystal Two and Crystal Too subsequently donned their walking shoes in the wondrous hamster city). This project left Boulder Journey School educators with many questions to ponder, foremost among them: Why did the construction of a special place for Crystal so compel the children?

Children have a fondness for finding and building special places. These childhood places lodge themselves so securely in our memories that as adults, we tend to recall them with smiles and inward gazes that transport us through time and space. (Readers might try this for themselves—What comes to mind when you think of *your* special childhood place?) The children's book *Roxaboxen* conveys a sense of childhood places being forever available for a visit because they always exist in our memories (McLerran, 1991).

Numerous researchers have studied adult memories of childhood places in order to understand better why these places remain salient across our life span. Part of the answer lies in the sense of refuge these places provide. In an adult-centered world where children often feel powerless, childhood places inspire a sense of security and control. They fulfill children's desire to take a break from the rush of activity around them, and from the demands of the adult world; they offer a space for children to pour out their troubles and achieve a sense of peace (Korpela, Kytta, & Hartig, 2002). Although children often escape alone, their special places also may serve as a meeting ground for fellow children (Zeegers, Readdick, & Hansen-Gandy, 1994). Alone or together, children enter these places to transcend their present lives; they pretend and dream, they clarify to themselves and to others who they really are, and they become more able to surmount the trials of childhood (Dovey, 1990). Adults dedicated to honoring and respecting children also must find ways to honor children's right to spaces of their own.

A FORT OF ONE'S OWN

Yi-Fu Tuan (1977) observed that the word *place* has two overlapping meanings: It refers both to a location in space *and* to a person's place in the social world. Furthermore, Tuan observed that one's position in the social world sets the boundaries for the physical spaces one can occupy. A consequence of the connection between place in society and physical space is that members of marginalized groups often have trouble finding places to call their own. In one of the classic texts on women's liberation, the essay *A Room of One's Own*, Virginia Woolf (1929/1991) asserted that no woman writer matched Shakespeare's prolific and inventive output because women had no claims to space—they had no property of their own—they were the property of their husbands. Without a place of their own from which to develop the personal point of view essential to writing, women could not compose and articulate their own ideas. Woolf concluded, "A lock on the door means the power to think for oneself" (p. 117).

In today's world, children find themselves in a similar situation—without spaces of their own. Children "live and act in environments planned and monitored by adults" (Kylin, 2003; see also Gutman & de Coninck-Smith, 2008). As discussed in previous chapters, young children are relegated to the home, but even within the houses where they spend most of their days, children have few claims to space. In one study of families with young children, researchers found that parents viewed themselves as homeowners and permanent residents, and viewed their children as temporary inhabitants. Furthermore, the youngest family members, that is, those most confined to the home, had the fewest claims to private space (Shamgar-Handleman & Belkin, 1984). Many schools also fail to offer children spaces of their own. Research suggests that just as homes are seen as the property of parents, children perceive their schools as the property of teachers (Yamamoto, 1979).

One outcome of children's lack of a claim to space is that adults rarely consult them about the design and utilization of the spaces they inhabit together (Schiavo, 1990). The rare instances when they *do* make decisions tend to be salient and memorable for children (Tognoli & Horwitz, 1982). Research suggests that if children did have input, they would claim more spaces for their own. In a study in which children designed their ideal homes, more than half enhanced their privacy by assigning a private bedroom, bathroom, or study to themselves, or by locating their rooms on different floors from their parents and siblings (Schiavo, 1990).

The authors have discussed the importance of facilitating children's participation in the "adult" world, but children also have the right to withdraw from this world. Children have a right to both participation and nonparticipation (Greenman, 2005a), and a right to withdraw from public and have their privacy honored. The United Nations Convention on the Rights of the Child recognizes these dual rights. While Article 12 affirms children's right to participation, Article 16 affirms children's right to privacy: "No child shall be subjected to arbitrary or unlawful interference with his or her privacy, family, home, or correspondence" (Office of the United Nations High Commission for Human Rights, 1989). In their development of a "mosaic approach" to listening to young children, Alison Clark and Peter Moss (2001) also warned of the "pitfalls of listening" (p. 61). Adults can assert power over children, both by rendering them invisible *and also* by requiring communication.

During the construction of Crystal's city, Boulder Journey School faculty realized that even young children are concerned about issues of privacy. The children involved in this project discussed with great animation the possibility of including a "secret passageway." They debated whether they needed to be able to see Crystal at all times to ensure her safety, or if the sometimes reclusive hamster should have a place in which she could conceal herself from view.

In constructing Crystal's city, the children recognized both the importance of participation in the larger and sometimes dangerous "outside" world, and the importance of a calm, reassuring haven into which one could escape alone. Researchers studying children's special places also have remarked on the importance of private and safe havens. David Sobel (1993) wrote, "As the notion of the self starts to mature in middle childhood, children start to perceive how fragile their individuality is in the face of the big world outside. The small, manageable world of the fort, with everything pulled inside, is calm and reassuring" (p. 74).

To some degree, children's need for small and protected places of their own reflects their place in the larger society where they may feel overwhelmed and invisible. A consideration of the nature of children's special places provides insight into the place of children in our society, and perhaps can help us to ensure that children's places are places of respect.

CHARACTERISTICS OF CHILDREN'S PLACES

Children lay claim to all sorts of spaces. Young children might take up residence in a nook behind the drapes, or be drawn to the back of a kitchen cupboard, seeking privacy amid the flurry of household activity. By the age of 7, children have graduated to places beyond the family living areas (Sobel, 1993), such as a cozy crawl space in the attic. By this age, they more often claim spaces in nature as well, like a labyrinth clipped through a hydrangea bush in the yard or a cluster of rocks alongside a nearby stream.

Perhaps the most important feature of children's spaces is that children are in control of them. Very young children exert control in the very act of *choosing* a place of their own. In a study of children's territories in day care settings (Zeegers et al., 1994), researchers asked the children whether they had a special place, and then asked, "Did you choose this place or did someone give it to you?" Of the 58 children who had a special place, 40 had chosen their space for themselves. One 4-1/2-year-old girl indicated the spot at the lunch table where she always sat as her special place, explaining, "I picked it myself" (p. 7).

Although children claim a variety of spaces, children's special places tend to have several features in common, all of which center on the importance of children being in control of their space. Children's spaces: (1) are defined by children, not by adults; (2) have thresholds that the children manage; and (3) contain a single child or small group of children, but not adults. Each of these features is described in more detail below.

Children Define the Space for Themselves

Regardless of whether children's special places are in the house, in the yard, in a field, or in the school, children prefer spaces as untouched and undefined by adults as possible. Thus, children's places tend to be abandoned, neglected, and/or wild.

Undefined spaces are available for children to alter however they see fit. Roger Hart (1979) observed that young children's first special places are found places. As children develop, their spaces are more often built constructions. In his groundbreaking study of children's places, Hart (1979) concluded, "One particularly important quality of environments for children is its suitability for modification by them" (p. 349). Children, like adults, make themselves comfortable in an environment by imposing their own order on it. Thus, children can use their spaces to try out ideas, to experiment. The British planner Robin Moore (1986) observed that children need spaces they can deconstruct and reconstruct continually in order to gain an understanding of the built world. He asked, "Where is this vital activity to be carried on if every part of the child's environment is spoken for to meet the economic, social, and cultural needs of the adult community?" (cited in Trimble, 1994, p. 27). Providing children with preformed playhouses and other adult-made spaces runs counter to children's need to make the space their own by transforming it (Olwig, 1990).

Children's need for spaces undefined by adults became evident in a Boulder Journey School project that took place in a class of 2-1/2- to 3-year-olds. In order to explore children's use of private spaces, teachers moved apart two classroom cabinets, creating a new space between them, and observed how children used this space (Figure 6.1).

Over the first few days children built in this space, filled it with objects, ran through it, and turned it into an airplane, a house, and a ghost train (Figure 6.2). The teachers queried the children about this evolving space and asked them, "What could this space be?" (Jagow, 2007). Cole provided an answer, the profundity of which soon would become clear. He responded, "Every kind of space."

The teachers in this classroom continued their efforts to pin down "what kind of space" this could be with the children's input. They experimented with the design by replacing the boards on top of the cabinets with a grey fabric roof (Figure 6.3). When the teachers experimented with design changes of their own making, the children soon lost interest in this once vital space, and the teachers remembered Cole's words. One of the teachers reflected:

> Was Cole telling me that when the space was bare and had yet to have a permanent definition, it was "every kind of space"—a space that could be open to interpretation and subject to change daily depending on both the internal and external needs of the child? This causes me to wonder if adults feel a need to define all of their spaces and in turn somewhat force children to define their spaces. Does this needlessly take away from the creativity and imagination of children and their abilities to transform the world and spaces around them? (Jagow, 2007)

FIGURE 6.1. A private, undefined space created for children to explore. © Boulder
   Journey School, 2010.

   In addition to choosing and modifying spaces, children define spaces for
themselves through naming their spaces. In David Sobel's (1993) study of children's special places, one adult recalled a crawl space she had claimed as her own.
She cleaned it out and painted it, and soon "it became apparent that it needed a
name. 'I am going to the crawl-space' just didn't cut it. It became 'the Hole' and
became a place to play alone or with a friend" (p. 93).

   Modifying and naming spaces both involve an exertion of will and imagination. For children, there is a strong link between creativity and claims of space.
During a Boulder Journey School project about private spaces, 3-year-old George
announced that his special place was "in my imagination." When 3-year-old Laurel was asked to draw her special place, the drawing itself became special. She
drew a border around her design and asserted, "See this long, long line? It's so
people don't get into my drawing because it's a secret" (Figure 6.4).

**FIGURE 6.2. Children built a variety of structures in the undefined space. ©
Boulder Journey School, 2010.**

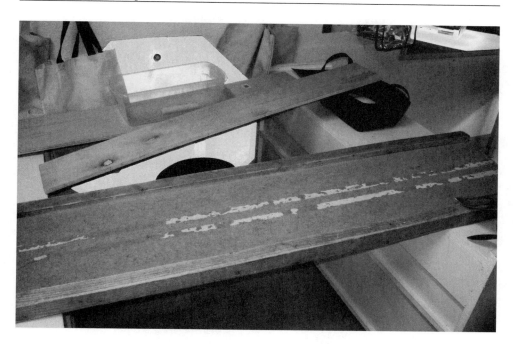

As another example of claiming space through creative acts, consider Figure 6.5, a photograph taken by 2-1/2-year-old Dylan. When this child saw her photograph, she exclaimed, "My sky!"

When children seek spaces undefined by adults to feed their souls, they often journey into nature (e.g., Louv, 2005). Natural spaces, unlike spaces built by adults, are inherently unclaimed and undefined. As a child in David Sobel's (1993) study reported, "The woods are my home and the house is my parents' house" (p. 125). The woods and other natural spaces are the domain of childhood. It is interesting to note that research shows a bias toward remembering more time spent in outdoor places than the actual amount of time spent there (Dovey, 1990). Howard Gardner (1999) observed, "Just as most ordinary children readily master language at an early age, so too are most children predisposed to explore the world of nature" (p. 50). Perhaps this is one reason why adults often use metaphors of nature when referring to young children who grow like *weeds*, who attend kinder*garten*, and who *blossom* into maturity.

Research suggests that children have a deep and direct connection to the natural world (Louv, 2005; Sebba 1991). While adults often view nature as a background for events, children tend to put nature in the foreground of their experience. In the book *The Geography of Childhood*, Gary Nabhan (1994) noted that adults interested in documenting the natural world scanned "the land for picturesque panoramas and scenic overlooks . . . while the kids were on their hands and knees, engaged with what was immediately before them" (p. 5). As a result, children's

FIGURE 6.3. Teachers experimented with the design of the undefined space. ©
Boulder Journey School, 2010.

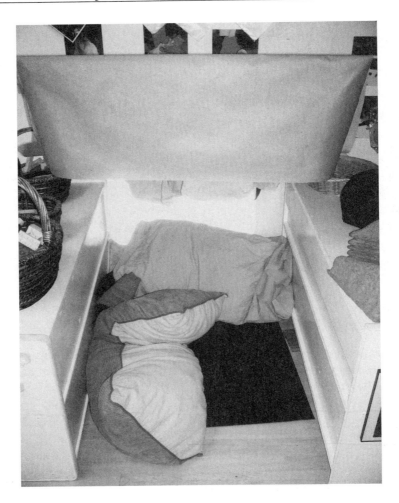

photographs featured "crisp close-ups of sagebrush lizards, yuccas, rock art, and
sister's funny faces. The few obligatory views of expansive canyons seemed, by
contrast, blurred and poorly framed" (p. 6).

Because nature is alive, it enlivens children and adults. Close contact with nature stimulates creativity and imagination (Cobb, 1959; Louv, 2005). Unlike adult-
created spaces, nature encourages children to be their own protagonists and to lay-
er their own meanings onto undefined space. Virginia Woolf generated the ideas
for her revolutionary essay, *A Room of One's Own*, on the banks of a river amid the
fire-colored bushes and lamenting willow trees. As a more personal example, a
seed of this book took root on a hike through the mountains of Colorado.

In Boulder, Colorado, the towering mountains are a prominent and significant
feature in the lives of many of the adults and children who live here. In the Boul-

FIGURE 6.4. A 3-year-old child's drawing of her special place. © Boulder Journey School, 2010.

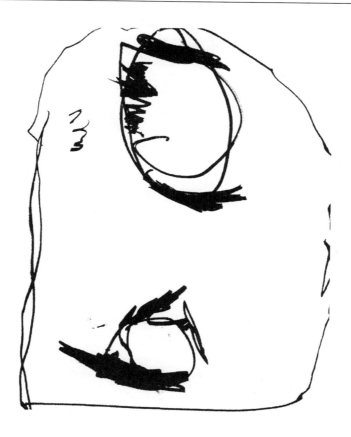

"See this long, long line? It's so people don't get into
my drawing because it's a secret"
-Laurel

der Journey School Charter on Children's Rights, children recognized the importance of mountains, asserting, "Children have a right to climb mountains, ski on
the mountains (when there is snow), and play on the mountains (because the
mountains are there for all of us to use)." The mountain emerged as an important
metaphor for freedom in the construction of Crystal's city (see Chapter 5). The importance of mountains also emerged in a subsequent study of children's privacy
and special places. The following exchange occurred after 3-year-old Aidan agreed
to draw a picture of his private place:

Aidan: That's the mountain.
Teacher: Is the mountain your special private place?
Aidan: All the mountains.

FIGURE 6.5. A 2-1/2-year-old child's photograph: "My sky!" © Boulder Journey School, 2010.

FIGURE 6.6. A 4-year-old child's drawing of the bedroom, featuring a door © Boulder Journey School, 2010.

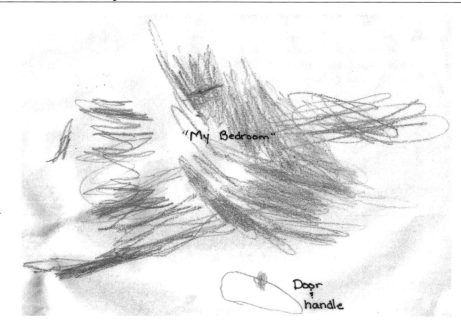

Children's Spaces Often Have Thresholds

For many children who claim or construct a private space, the establishment of a boundary is crucial. "People who value privacy cross thresholds that signal others not to follow" (Peterson, 1992, p. 29). This explains why the drawing Laurel made of her special place (Figure 6.4) required a line around it to keep people out. In a Swedish study of children's *kojor,* which loosely translates as "dens," Maria Kylin (2003) found the dens always included some sort of boundary, or threshold, that separated the space from the rest of the world. Access to the den required a ritual passage, such as pressing a special stick to gain entrance. (Note that secret passwords serve a similar threshold-maintaining function.) The passageway to the *kojor* could be as simple as two crossed sticks, or something much more elaborate, like loops woven from grass to ensnare the feet of intruders, or deep holes that intruders would fall into. "One child's ingenious rope trap was built high up between branches so that an adult would be caught, but a child could go under" (Kylin, 2003, p. 15).

In David Sobel's (1993) study of the places claimed by elementary school children in Devon, England, one boy described a secret island he had claimed. The boy had widened the stream at the entranceway, and in a nearby bush he hid a board for his own crossing of the water. To further deter invaders, he also built a trap by covering the trickling stream with leaves so that it would appear solid, but anyone trying to approach the island would fall into the water.

Some research suggests that treetops figure prominently in children's landscapes, perhaps because the very act of climbing a tree involves the crossing of a threshold—the barrier from land to sky. When a child climbs a tree, he or she achieves a "vertical separation from everyday life" (Dovey, 1990, p. 16). In the construction of Crystal's city, vertical separation was also important. Children consistently positioned the hamster's private haven above her city of adventure. Although vertical separation is usually upward, it can be downward as well. Three year-old Kaden drew his ideal special place and described it as follows: "It would go down, down, down. To get up you'd climb on the ladder."

Vertical separation may require ladders, and ladders did appear frequently in the design of Crystal's city. In addition to ladders, stairs, and even elevators, the children frequently drew doors as a means of distinguishing between public and private worlds. Because control over the threshold is crucial to a sense of privacy, the children repeatedly asserted the importance of Crystal being able to open and close the door herself.

Crystal needs a door. Maybe when the door shuts, she can open it. Then she can go in her bedroom.

Then we can make a doorway so she can open and close it herself.

The importance of doors also emerged in a Boulder Journey School study of children's bedrooms. Previous research has shown that when young children are

FIGURE 6.7. A 4-year-old child's drawing of the bedroom, with an oversized, centrally located door. © Boulder Journey School, 2010.

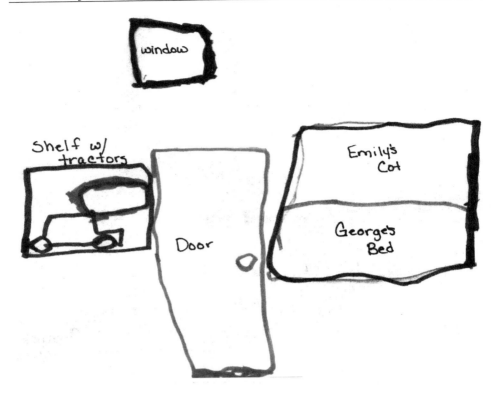

asked to draw their favorite places to play, the home appears more commonly than any other space (Moore & Young, 1978). Children from preschool through high school designate their bedrooms as their favorite room in the house (Schiavo, 1987). When 4-year-olds at Boulder Journey School were asked to draw pictures of their bedrooms, they almost always included doors. Sometimes it was the only distinctive feature, as in Figures 6.6 and 6.7. Or, the importance of the door as a part of the room's boundary was highlighted, as in Figure 6.8.

In the aforementioned study in which Boulder Journey School teachers separated two cabinets to create a new children's space, the importance of thresholds was immediately apparent (Figure 6.9). One of the teachers recalls that within the first few days of the new space's existence:

> I observed Cooper in Room 2 take a stop sign and balance it on its end so that it would stand up and block the entrance into the new private space we had created. The space was still completely bare at this time and yet Cooper showed through his actions that a threshold to the space was important to him and a desired addition. Over the semester, I continuously observed children making their own thresholds like Cooper did with the stop sign. Thresholds were made with blankets, pillows, and boards almost daily as the space transformed into tents and forts. (Jagow, 2007)

FIGURE 6.8. A 4-year-old child's drawing of the bedroom, with the door as part of the bedroom's boundary. © Boulder Journey School, 2010.

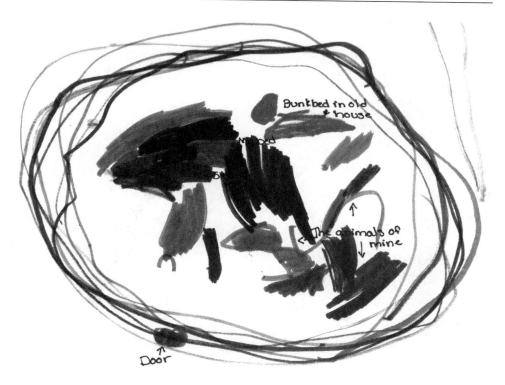

The addition of a curtain to the space between the cabinets led to another insight about thresholds. Children in this classroom had developed a game in which they pretended to be animals. After establishing the curtain as a threshold, the children realized that transforming into an animal behind the curtain and emerging "in character" added to their enjoyment of the animal game (Figure 6.10).

Children showed great interest in using the space between the cabinets as a place to explore their identities. They asked that the space include mirrors, and spent much of their time gazing at their reflections either alone or with a friend (Figure 6.11).

Children's Spaces Are for Children: Either Alone or Together

In their special places, children negotiate the line between secret/private and social/public. The psychologist Irwin Altman (1975) proposed a dialectic view of privacy, which emphasizes the importance of boundaries as the individual seeks to balance social interaction and restriction of interaction. The importance of this dialectic to young children may account for the popularity of interactive games such as peek-a-boo and hide-and-seek, games in which children delight in the excitement of both hiding and uncovering in the presence of others (Figure 6.12).

FIGURE 6.9. Children created thresholds for their space. © Boulder Journey School, 2010.

Key to a dialectic view of privacy is control over access (Wolfe, 1978). Having this control reduces one's sense of vulnerability (Margulis, 1977, 2003). Thus, children need private spaces, not solely or most importantly in order to be alone, but because such spaces provide children with a sense of autonomy and power in relation to others, especially adults.

In their private places, children can be completely alone, or they can escape from the adult world *with friends.* In a study of children's territories in a day care setting, one 5-year-old child claimed as his special place an 18-inch crawl space underneath a playhouse, which he chose because "I can get under there and hide by myself, but sometimes my friend comes too" (Zeegers et al., 1994, p. 6). The size of the space precluded, however, entrance by adults. An appealing group of boxes on a Boulder Journey School playground allowed children to hide both alone and together—they could each have their own box, or hide as a group (Figure 6.13).

In the study of dens in Sweden, Maria Kylin (2003) found that just as children differ in sociability, their dens also "range between 'very secret' and 'very social' but both aspects are always present to some extent" (p. 24). While some children prefer to inhabit special places completely alone, others choose to escape from adult gazes with friends. In one drawing created by a social 4-year-old as part of the Boulder Journey School study of children's bedrooms, friends are the only features the child drew within the boundary of her bedroom (Figure 6.14).

FIGURE 6.10. Establishing the curtain as a threshold from which to emerge "in character." © Boulder Journey School, 2010.

It appears that as children grow older, they more often seek the company of friends in their special places (R. Hart, 1979; Wolfe, 1978). Children also become increasingly interested in creating rules for their space. When one has claim to a space, one gets to decide what happens within that space, as evidenced in the parental adage, "You'll do as I say as long as you live under my roof." When small groups of children find or build roofs of their own, considerable energy may go into deciding what happens under those roofs. One study of schoolyards in the United States found that the forts children built often passed from older to younger children, along with a complex system of rules that constituted a strong and hierarchical "fort culture" (Powell, 2001, cited in Kylin, 2003).

Initially, young children's escape from adult control and their autonomy in making decisions may matter more than the rules themselves. When my older son Asher was 3 and unhappy with *always* having to go along with the grown-ups, our family came up with the idea of having 1 day a week during which he could make the decisions about where we went, what we ate, and so on. He could, if he chose, have chocolate cake for dinner. Surprisingly, on "Asher Day," my son usually opted to save chocolate cake for dessert, and family activities greatly resembled activities that occurred on the other 6 days of the week with one key difference: Only on "Asher Day" did my son ask his parents what *we* wanted to do.

FIGURE 6.11. Children spent much of their time gazing at their reflections, either alone or with a friend. © Boulder Journey School, 2010.

FIGURE 6.12. A photograph of a hiding child, taken by a 3-year-old photographer. © Boulder Journey School, 2010.

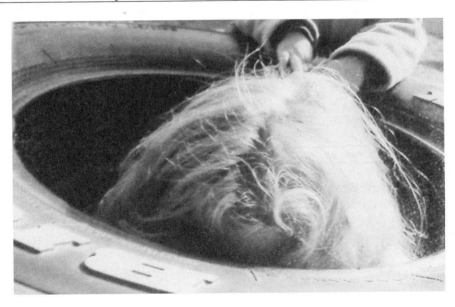

FIGURE 6.13. Boxes are for hiding, both alone and together. © Boulder Journey School, 2010.

As children gain experience in generating their own rules, chidren's culture becomes increasingly self-sustaining and refined. This is not to say that children generate their cultures out of nothing. William Damon (1988) found that children gain from adults "knowledge of the social order, prescribed social rules, and the moral rationales behind them," while in the context of peer relationships, children learn processes of negotiation that enable them to "work out moral rules democratically with others all through life" (p. 86). By establishing rules of relating within the more equitable social grouping of peers, "children enter and become active in a wider community, outside the family, co-constructing with children their own cultural forms . . . and increasing their sphere of social influence" (Moss & Petrie, 2002, p. 104).

CONCLUSION

The marginalized social position of children, and their consequent lack of place in the larger society, helps explain children's interest in finding and building small, hidden spaces for themselves. To some degree, other marginalized groups also seek out safe havens. The singer, scholar, and activist Bernice Johnson Reagon (1981/1992) noted the importance of secluded places for people who feel invisible or unvalued in society. She explained that in such spaces "you take the time to try to construct within yourself and within your community who you would be if

FIGURE 6.14. A 4-year-old child's drawing of her bedroom that features her friends. © Boulder Journey School, 2010.

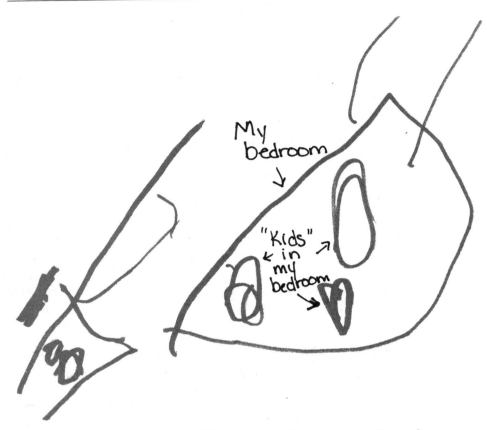

you were running society" (p. 505). Although Reagon was talking about women in general, and women of color in particular, her comments ring true for children's communities as well.

Perhaps one reason why childhood spaces live on so powerfully in adult memories is because the selves and the societies constructed alone and with other children in childhood spaces really do live on in adulthood. Childhood places are reflections of the present as well as rehearsals of the future. They are early examples of the communities people co-create across the lifespan. As author Judith Rich Harris (1998) put it:

> Children are not incompetent members of the adults' society: they are competent members of their own society, which has its own standards and its own culture . . . loosely based on the majority culture within which it exists. But it adapts the majority culture to its own purposes and it includes elements that are lacking in the adult culture. (p. 199)

In the United States, adults are wary of child-only spaces. In contrast, many Nordic day care centers have spaces designated as child-only in which adults cannot trespass (Wagner, 2004). Although children in these spaces do engage in activities that adults tend to interrupt, such as pillow fights, the behaviors are not unduly dangerous.

Play theorist Brian Sutton-Smith (1990) argued for the importance of unregulated, recurrent social occasions (such as recess) where a "tribe of children" can associate freely. The use of the term *tribe* suggests a lack of civilization, perhaps conjuring images from William Golding's (1954) book *Lord of the Flies*. It may be the case, however, that child-only spaces actually promote children's civilization. Toward this goal, it is incumbent upon adults to build the trust that allows children control over their own spaces. Most likely, children will build their own communities upon the most useful foundations of what adults have offered to them. Adults can foster the development of a supportive and respectful children's culture by embodying support and respect in our own relationships with children and others. As Erik Erikson wrote in 1965:

> It is the young who, by their responses and actions, tell the old whether life as represented by the old and as presented to the young has meaning; and it is the young who carry in them the power to confirm those who confirm them and, joining the issues, to renew and to regenerate, or to reform and to rebel. (p. 24)

For Further Thought

1. To what extent do you believe in the importance of children's right to privacy? When and how might you and other adults support children's right to nonparticipation?

2. Recall the places you spent your time as a child. Did you have a special place? If so, draw/describe this place and how it made you feel. In what ways was your special place similar to and/or different than the special places described in this chapter (e.g., was it connected to nature, were adults excluded)?

3. Examine the idea of child-centered spaces and communities as compared with those of adults. How are they the same and how are they different? How can adults support children's spaces and communities? Do adults need to give up adult spaces in order to provide spaces for children?

4. Looking across all of the chapters, what do you see as *your* next step in promoting children's rights? What concrete action(s) have you taken or do you plan to take?

Conclusion

In writing this book, the authors hope to encourage readers to explore, appreciate, and articulate ideas about young children's rights. We also hope to inspire reflection and provoke discussion. Informed discussion augments our collective understanding of children's rights and allows the children's rights movement to advance. Debate is necessary, and even the like-minded authors, children, families, and faculty involved in bringing this book to fruition have and continue to debate a number of key questions, such as:

- What are the limits around children's right to participate in society? Should children vote, discuss sexuality, learn about and play war, watch the news, and attend funerals?
- To what extent should adults encourage children's fantasies? Does nurturing children's beliefs in cultural myths, such as the tooth fairy or Santa Claus, betray our commitment to truth-telling and disrespect children's ability to reason? Or does it support children's sense of wonder?
- Under what circumstances should adults require children to engage in activities the children would not choose? Should children decide whether or not to go to church regularly or practice a musical instrument?

Although questions about children's rights continue to persist, this book offers principles that may help to address them. A few key principles are highlighted below.

1. Questions surrounding children's rights deserve open and honest consideration among adults, among children and adults, and among children. One of the main ideas of this book, an idea around which all others coalesce, is that adults must listen to children. Our emphasis on listening first appears in the book's title, and every chapter reinforces this notion. Children should be neither invisible nor silent. Honoring children's voices means that children have a say, especially in issues that affect them. This does *not* mean children decide issues. It does mean children's perspectives always matter. This book has offered numerous guidelines for listening, such as:

- Accommodate disturbance to one's own views—be willing to learn and change as a result of encounters with children.
- Offer opportunities for children to communicate using verbal and nonverbal languages.
- Listen patiently. Allow children the space and time to participate.
- Recognize that dialogues about rights are ongoing and evolving and ideas change.
- Embrace disagreement and conflict. Consider the ways that children's understanding and expression of conflict differ from adults' ways.
- Talk to children within a relevant context. Make ideas real and concrete rather than abstract.
- Question internalized models of how adults *should* behave.
- Recognize gaps between one's ideals (e.g., all people are created equal) and one's behavior.
- Explore the ways in which documentation can facilitate understanding.

Transformative dialogues occur when adults believe that children have valuable contributions to make, which leads to a second principle.

2. *Images of children as vulnerable, unformed, and untrustworthy must be replaced with images of children as capable and competent. Furthermore, treating children as capable and competent supports them in both expressing and enhancing their competence.* The stories in the book highlight the competence, capabilities, and creativity of young children. Children also can be trusted. They want to do the right thing and usually make good decisions.

Fear often leads us to limit children's rights—fear of out-of-control children and also fear of an out-of-control world. Adults' desire to protect children from harsh realities must exist alongside a realization that children may know more than we give them credit for. Adults' failure to acknowledge children's awareness of reality can leave children feeling alone and unsupported, instead of protected from the harsh realities of life. Adults can best rear future, civic-minded citizens by standing alongside children, and offering whatever assistance we can as they negotiate their place in the present. This suggests that adults:

- Convey to children, through words and actions, that their voices are important and respected.
- Recognize that overprotection entails its own risks.
- Scaffold children's participation. Adults can use our resources, such as life experience, access to information, and facility with verbal expression, to help children participate. Or, if this power is abused, to silence them.

- Encourage children to engage in their own processes of discovery and meaning-making rather than taking them over. Adults continually must consider whether a situation calls for stepping in or stepping out.

Children are inherently social beings, who benefit from making ideas and participating in community life with adults and with other children. This suggests a third principle:

3. Children's relationships with other children enhance their ability to participate. It is time to rethink the view of children as egocentric. Evidence has accumulated that children are acutely sensitive to the perspectives of others. In addition, interdependence can be seen as a goal of development, along with greater autonomy. Adult society often has faulted children for a lack of community-mindedness, while simultaneously removing them from adult society and communities of children. Children deserve access to communities, including communities where they do not find themselves in a subordinate position. Alderson (2000b) noted that children learn well "especially in small groups and away from strong relationships of authority and dependence" (p. 131). Similarly, Mayall (2000b) noted that children in groups are better able to assert their own perspectives while in the presence of adult social power. Children, like other marginalized groups, find strength in numbers. Thus, adults must:

- Provide opportunities for children to offer collective, as well as individual, voices.
- Resist temptation to use adult power to disrupt peer relationships.
- Cultivate spaces that support children's participation.

4. Rights are not conditional, nor are they a zero-sum entity. Melton (2009) recently warned against discussions of rights that focus on the need to achieve balance, whether a balance between protection and participation, or rights and responsibilities, or parents' rights and children's rights. He noted that such relativism runs counter to the universalism that is at the heart of the notion of *rights*. "Like the international human rights instruments that preceded it, the Convention on the Rights of the Child is based on 'recognition of the inherent dignity and of the equal and inalienable rights of all members of the human family'" (p. 903). In other words, people do not *earn* rights. They possess rights by virtue of their humanity.

A children's rights perspective is surely limited by the notion that when children receive more rights, adults get fewer. Just as love is self-perpetuating—the more we give away, the more we find available—so, too, can a world exist in which respect grows to encircle us all, children and adults alike.

IT HAS BEEN SAID that every ending is also a beginning. Hopefully, as readers prepare to turn the last page of this book, they will find themselves at a new starting point. This is an exciting moment in history. In the time it has taken to write this book, the number of articles, Web sites, books, and conferences dedicated to supporting children's rights has exploded. The movement for children's rights continues to gain momentum. Readers who take on the struggle for children's rights join an ever-growing group of dedicated researchers, educators, parents, policymakers, and most important, children. Martin Luther King, Jr. (1967) observed that "the arc of the moral universe is long but it bends toward justice." The march toward greater respect for and equality with children is unstoppable. This book succeeds if it has offered some insights and tools that fellow marchers find useful.

References

Adams, M., Bell, L., & Griffin, P. (1997). *Teaching for diversity and social justice: A source-book for teachers and trainers.* New York: Routledge.

Alderson, P. (1994). Researching children's rights to integrity. In B. Mayall (Ed.), *Children's childhoods observed and experienced* (pp. 45–62). London: Falmer Press.

Alderson, P. (2000a). Children as researchers: The effects of participation rights on research methodology. In P. Christensen & A. James (Eds.), *Research with children: Perspectives and practices* (pp. 241–257). London: Falmer Press.

Alderson, P. (2000b). *Young children's rights: Exploring beliefs, principles, and practices.* London: Jessica Kingsley.

Altman, I. (1975). *The environment and social behavior.* Monterey, CA: Brooks/Cole.

Ariès, Philippe. (1962). *Centuries of childhood: A social history of family life.* New York: Vintage Books.

Arrieta, G., & Cheynut, A. (2002, May 8). United Nations Special Session on Children, Message from the Children's Forum. Retrieved March 14, 2005, from http://www.unicef.org/specialsession/documentation/childrens-statement.htm

Assor, A., Roth, G., & Deci, E. (2004). The emotional costs of parents' conditional regard: A self-determination theory analysis. *Journal of Personality, 72,* 47–89.

Bandman, B. (1999) *Children's right to freedom, care, and enlightenment.* New York: Garland.

Bateson, M. C. (2000). *Full circles, overlapping lives.* New York: Random House.

Baumrind, D. (1966). Effects of authoritative parental control on child behavior. *Child Development, 37*(4), 887–907.

Baumrind, D. (1967). Child care practices anteceding three patterns of preschool behavior. *Genetic Psychology Monographs, 75*(1), 43–88.

Bayer, C. L., Whaley, K. L., & May, S. E. (1995). Strategic assistance in toddler disputes: Sequences and patterns of teachers' message strategies. *Early Education and Development, 6*(4), 405–432.

Bellah, R. N., Madsen, R., Sullivan, W. M., Swidler, A., & Tipton, S. M. (1985). *Habits of the heart: Individualism and commitment in American life.* New York: Harper & Row.

Berman, S. (1997). *Children's social consciousness and the development of social responsibility.* Albany: State University of New York Press.

Bowlby, J. (1980). *Attachment and loss: Vol. 2. Separation.* New York: Basic Books. (Original published 1973)

Bridges, R. (1999). *Through my eyes.* New York: Scholastic Press.

Cherney, I., & Perry, N. W. (1996). Children's attitudes toward their rights: An international perspective. In E. Verhellen (Ed.), *Monitoring children's rights* (pp. 241–250). The Netherlands: Kluwer Law International.

Clark, A., & Moss, P. (2001). *Listening to young children: The mosaic approach.* London: National Children's Bureau.

Clarkson, E. (2004). Unpublished manuscript. Boulder Journey School, Boulder, CO.

Cobb, E. (1959). The ecology of imagination in childhood. *Daedalus, 88,* 537–548.

Cone, J. (1991). *Martin & Malcolm & America.* Maryknoll, NY: Orbis Books.

Da Ros, D. A., & Kovach, B. A. (1998). Assisting toddlers and caregivers during conflict resolutions: Interactions that promote socialization. *Childhood Education, 75*(I), 25–30.

Dahlberg, G., Moss, P., & Pence, E. (1999). *Beyond quality in early childhood education and care.* London: Routledge.

Damon, W. (1988) *The moral child.* New York: Free Press.

Dawe, H. C. (1934). An analysis of two hundred quarrels of preschool children. *Child Development, 5,* 139–157.

Doherty-Sneddon, G. (2003). *Children's unspoken language.* Philadelphia: Jessica Kingsley.

Dovey, K. (1990). Refuge and imagination: Places of peace in childhood. *Children's Environment Quarterly, 7*(2) 13–17.

Edwards, C. (1995, October 16–17). Democratic participation in a community of learners: Loris Malaguzzi's philosophy of education as relationship. Lecture prepared for "Nostalgia del futuro: Liberare speranze per uno nuova cultura dell'infanzia," an international seminar to consider the educational contributions of Loris Malaguzzi, Milan. Retrieved February 2, 2008, from http://digitalcommons.unl.edu/cgi/viewcontent.cgi?article=1014&context=famconfacpub

Edwards, C., Gandini, L., & Forman, G. (1998). *The hundred languages of children: The Reggio Emilia approach— Advanced reflections.* Westport, CT: Ablex.

Eisenberg, N. (1982). *The development of prosocial behavior.* New York: Academic Press.

Eisenberg, N. (1986). *Altruistic emotion, cognition, and behavior.* Hillsdale, NJ: Erlbaum.

Eisenberg, N. (1992). *The caring child.* Cambridge, MA: Harvard University Press.

Elkind, D. (1988). *The hurried child* (rev. ed). Reading, MA: Addison-Wesley.

Ellison, R. (1947). *Invisible man.* New York: Vintage Books.

Erikson, E. (1965). Youth: Fidelity and diversity. In E. Erikson (Ed.), *The challenge of youth* (p. 128). Garden City, NY: Anchor.

Etzioni, A. (1993). *The spirit of community: The reinvention of American society.* New York: Touchstone.

Etzioni, A. (1996). *The new golden rule: Community and morality in a democratic society.* New York: Basic Books.

Farson, R. (1974). *Birthrights: A bill of rights for children.* New York: Macmillan.

Fine, M., & Asch, A. (1988). Disability beyond stigma: Social interaction, discrimination, and activism. *Journal of Social Issues, 44,* 3–21.

Firestone, S. (1972). *Dialectics of sex: The case for feminist revolution.* New York: Bantam.

Fraser, S., & Gestwicki, C. (2001). *Authentic childhood: Experiencing Reggio Emilia in the classroom.* Clifton Park, NY: CENGAGE Delmar Learning.

Freire, P. (1992). *Pedagogy of the oppressed.* New York: Continuum. (Original published 1972)

Freud, S. (1995). *The basic writings of Sigmund Freud* (A. A. Brill, Trans.). New York: Modern Library.

Friedan, B. (1963). *The feminine mystique.* New York: Norton.

Gans, R. (1952). John Dewey and the understanding of children. *Teachers College Record,* 136–138.

Gardner, H. (1999). *Intelligence reframed: Multiple intelligences for the 21st century.* New York: Basic Books.

Garrison, W. L. (1829). Address to the colonization society. Retrieved March 14, 2005, from http://teachingamericanhistory.org/library/index.asp?document=562

Giese, N. (2008). What's new: Adult and child brains perform tasks differently. Washington University Program in Neuroscience. Retrieved February 23, 2010, from http://neuroscience.wustl.edu/news/whatsnew23.html

Gilligan, C. (1982). *In a different voice: Psychological theory and women's development.* Camridge, MA: Harvard University Press.

Gini, A. (2003). *The importance of being lazy: In praise of play, leisure, and vacations.* London: Routledge.

Glass, T. A., Matchar, D. B., Belyea, M., & Feussner, J. R. (1993). Impact of social support on outcome in first stroke. *Stroke, 24,* 64–70.

Glassner, B. (2000). *The culture of fear: Why Americans are afraid of the wrong things.* New York: Basic Books.

Golding, W. (1954) *Lord of the flies.* New York: Berkeley.

Goldschmeid, E., & Jackson, S. (1994). *People under three: Young children in daycare.* London: Routledge.

Greenman, J. (2005a). *Caring spaces, learning places: Children's environments that work.* Redmond, WA: Exchange Press.

Greenman, J. (2005b, May). Places for childhood in the 21st century: A conceptual framework. *Journal of the National Association for the Education of Young Children.* Retrieved August 7, 2007, from http://www.journal.naeyc.org/btj/200505/01Greenman.asp

Gutman, M., & de Coninck-Smith, N. (Eds.). (2008). *Designing modern childhoods: History, space, and the material culture of children.* Piscataway, NJ: Rutgers University Press.

Hall, E., & Rudkin, J. K. (2003, January/February). Supportive social learning: Creating classroom communities that care. *Childcare Information Exchange, 149,* 12–16.

Harding, V. (1990). *Hope and history: Why we must share the story of the movement.* Maryknoll, NY: Orbis Books.

Harris, J. R. (1998). *The nurture assumption.* New York: Free Press.

Hart, R. (1979). *Children's experience of place.* New York: Irvington.

Hart, R. (1992). *Children's participation: From tokenism to citizenship* (Innocenti essays No. 4). Florence: UNICEF.

Hart, S., & Hodson, V. K. (2004). *The compassionate classroom*. Encinitas, CA: Puddle-Dancer Press.

Hart, S., Zeidner, M., & Pavlovic, Z. (1996). Children's rights: Cross-national research on perspectives of children and their teachers. In M. John (Ed.), *Children in charge: The child's right to a fair hearing* (pp. 38–55). London: Jessica Kingsley.

Hartup, W. W., & Laursen, B. (1991). Relationships as developmental contexts. In R. Cohen & A. W. Siegel (Eds.), *Context and development* (253279). Hillsdale, NJ: Erlbaum.

Hartup, W. W., Laursen, B., Stewart, H. L., & Eastenson, A. (1988). Conflict and friendship relations of young children. *Child Development, 59*, 1590–1600.

Hawkins, D. (1997). *Afterword*. In F. P. Lothrop Hawkins, *To journey with children*. Boulder: University of Colorado Press.

Heywood, C. (2001). *A history of childhood: Children and childhood in the West from medieval to modern times*. Malden, MA: Blackwell.

Hillman, I. (2003). Unpublished manuscript for Boulder Journey School.

Hillman, M., Adams, J., & Whitelegg, J. (1991). *One false move . . . A study of children's independent mobility*. London: Policy Studies Institute.

Hoffman, M. (1982). Development of prosocial motivation: Empathy and guilt. In N. Eisenberg (Ed.), *The development of prosocial behavior* (pp. 281–313). New York: Academic Press.

Hoffman, M. L. 2000. *Empathy and moral development: Implications for caring and justice*. Cambridge: Cambridge University Press.

hooks, b. (2000). *All about love*. New York: Morrow.

Howe, R. B, & Covell, K. (2005). *Empowering children: Children's rights education as a pathway to citizenship*. Toronto: University of Toronto Press.

Jagow, A. (2007). Unpublished manuscript for Boulder Journey School.

Johnson, H. B. (2003, November 23). The disability gulag. *New York Times Magazine*, pp. 59–64.

Jones, A. (1993). *Wade in the water: The wisdom of the spirituals*. Maryknoll, NY: Orbis Books.

Jones, E., & Reynolds, G. (1992). *The play's the thing: Teachers' roles in children's play*. New York: Teachers College Press.

Jones, J. (1994). Our similarities are different: Toward a psychology of affirmative diversity. In E. J. Trickett, R. J. Watts, & D. Birman (Eds.), *Human diversity: Perspectives on people in context* (pp. 27–45). San Francisco: Jossey-Bass.

Kagan, J. (1994). *The nature of the child* (10th anniversary ed.). New York: Basic Books.

Keller, H. (1957). *The open door*. New York: Doubleday.

Kielburger, C. (1998). *Free the children*. Toronto: McClelland & Stewart.

Killen, M., & Turiel, E. (1994). Conflict resolution in preschool social interaction. *Early Education and Development, 2*(4), 240–255.

King, M. L., Jr. (1967, August). Where do we go from here? Address to the Southern Christian Leadership Conference, Atlanta, GA. Available at http://www.afscme.

org/about/1549.cfm

Kjørholt, A. T. (2003). Imagined communities: The local community as a place for "children's culture" and social participation in Norway. In K. F. Olwig & E. Gulløw (Eds.), *Children's places: Cross-cultural perspectives* (pp. 197–216). London: Routledge.

Kleinman, S., & Menn, L. (1997). Shirley says: Living with aphasia. Retrieved August 11, 2009, from http://spot.colorado.edu/~menn/Shirley4.pdf

Kohlberg, L. (1981). *Essays on moral development.* San Francisco: Harper & Row.

Kohn, A. (2005). *Unconditional parenting: Moving from rewards and punishment to love and reason.* New York: Atria Books.

Korczak, J. (n. d.). Appendix: Janusz Korczak's Declaration of Children's Rights. Retrieved February 8, 2010, from http://korczak.com/Biography/kap-38.htm

Korpela, K., Kytta, M., & Hartig, T. (2002). Children's favorite places: Restorative experience, self-regulation and children's place preferences. *Journal of Environmental Psychology, 22,* 387–398.

Kylin, M. (2003). Creating dens. *Children, Youth, and Environments, 13*(1). Retrieved February 8, 2010, from http://colorado.edu/journals/cye/13_1/Voll3_1Articles/CYE_CurrentIssue_Article_Dens_Kylin.htm

Langsted, O. (1994). Looking at quality from the child's perspective. In P. Moss & A. Pence (Eds.), *Valuing quality in early childhood services* (pp. 28–42). New York: Teachers College Press.

Lansdown, G. (1994). Children's rights. In B. Mayall (Ed.), *Children's childhoods observed and experienced* (pp. 33–44). London: Falmer Press.

Lansdown, G. (1996). Respecting the right of children to be heard. In G. Pugh (Ed.), *Contemporary issues in the early years* (pp. 68–82). London: Paul Chapman.

Laursen, B., & Hartup, W. W. (1989). The dynamics of preschool children's conflicts. *Merrill-Palmer Quarterly, 35,* 281–297.

Levine, E. (1993). *Freedom's children: Young civil rights activists tell their own stories.* New York: Putnam's.

Lewis, C. C. (1996). Beyond conflict resolution skills: How do children develop the will to solve conflicts at school? In M. Killen (Ed.), *New directions in child development* (pp. 91–106). San Francisco: Jossey-Bass.

Lorde, A. (1984). Learning from the 60s. In *Sister outsider* (pp. 134–144). Freedom, CA: Crossing Press.

Louv, R. (2005). *Last child in the woods.* New York: Algonquin Books.

Maher, A., & Sieminski, J. (2006, June 22–24). Saturn 5: The largest rocket ship ever built. Presentation at the Boulder Journey School Summer Conference, An evolution of understanding: From daily moments to long-term investigations, Boulder, CO.

Margulis, S. T. (1977). Conceptions of privacy: Current status and next steps. *Journal of Social Issues, 33*(3), 5–21.

Margulis, S. T. (2003). Privacy as a social and behavioral concept. *Journal of Social Issues, 59,* 243–261.

Maruyama, M. (1983). Cross-cultural perspectives on social and community change. In E. Seidman (Ed.), *Handbook of social intervention* (pp. 33–47). Beverly Hills, CA: Sage.

Mayall, B. (2000a). Conversations with children: Working with generational issues. In P. Christensen & A. James (Eds.), *Research with children: Perspectives and practices* (pp. 120–135). London: Falmer Press.

Mayall, B. (2000b). The sociology of childhood: Children's autonomy and participation rights. In A. B. Smith, M. Gollop, K. Marshall, & K. Nairn (Eds.), *Advocating for children: International perspectives on children's rights* (pp. 126–140). Dunedin, New Zealand: Otago University Press.

Mayer, R. H. (2008). *When the children marched: The Birmingham civil rights movement.* Berkeley Heights, NJ: Enslow.

McKay, F. (1990). Discipline. In A. Stonehouse (Ed.), *Trusting toddlers: Planning for one-to-three year olds in child care centres* (pp. 65–78). St. Paul, MN: Redleaf Press.

McLeod, A. (2008). Listening to children: A practitioner's guide. London: Jessica Kingsley.

McLerran, A. (1991). *Roxaboxen.* New York: Lothrop, Lee & Shepard Books.

Melton, G. B. (1980). Children's concepts of their rights. *Journal of Clinical Child Psychology, 9,* 186–190.

Melton, G. B. (2009). Beyond balancing: Toward an integrated approach to children's rights. *Journal of Social Issues, 64*(4), 903–920.

Memmi, A. (1965. *The colonizer and the colonized.* Boston: Beacon Press.

Miljeteig, P. (2000). Children's democratic rights: Are we ready? What we can learn from young workers. In A. B. Smith, M. Gollop, K. Marshall, & K. Nairn (Eds), *Advocating for children: International perspectives on children's rights* (pp. 159–175). Dunedin, New Zealand: University of Otago Press.

Miller, A. (1983). *For your own good: Hidden cruelty in child-rearing and the roots of violence.* New York: Farrar, Strass, & Giroux.

Miller, D. L., & Challas, G. (1980). Intergenerational child abuse: A longitudinal study. Institute for Scientific Analysis. Retrieved August 7, 2007, from http://www.scientificanalysis.org/violence.html

Montessori, M. (1967). *The child.* Wheaton, IL: Theosophical Publishing House.

Mooney, C. G. (2000). *Theories of childhood: An introduction to Dewey, Montessori, Erikson, Piaget & Vygotsky.* St. Paul, MN: Redleaf Press.

Moore, R. (1986). *Childhood's domain.* London: Croom Helm.

Moore, R. C. (1997). The need for nature: A childhood right. *Social Justice, 24,* 203–221.

Moore, R., & Young, D. (1978). Childhood outdoors: Toward a social ecology of the landscape. In I. Altman & J. F. Wolwill (Eds.), *Human behavior and environment: Vol. 3. Children and the environment* (pp. 83–127). New York: Plenum.

Mooreshead, A. (2006).Unpublished manuscript for Boulder Journey School.

Moss, P., & Petrie, P. (2002). *Children's service to children's spaces: Public policy, children, and childhood.* London: Routledge/Falmer.

Municipality of Reggio Emilia Infant Toddler Centers and Preschools. (1999). *The municipal infant-toddler centers and preschools of Reggio Emilia: Historical notes and general information* (2nd ed.). Reggio Emilia, Italy: Reggio Children Srl.

Nabhan, G. P. (1994). A child's sense of wildness. In G. P. Nabhan & S. Trimble, *The geography of childhood: Why children need wild places* (pp. 3–14). Boston: Beacon Press.

Nabhan, G. P., & Trimble, S. (1994). *The geography of childhood: Why children need wild places.* Boston: Beacon Press.

Nutbrown, C. (2001). Watching and learning: The tools of assessment. In G. Pugh (Ed.), *Contemporary issues in the early years: Working collaboratively with children* (3rd ed., pp. 66–77). London: Paul Chapman.

Oakley, A. (1994). Women and children first and last: Parallels and differences between children's and women's studies. In B. Mayall (Ed.), *Children's childhoods observed and experienced* (pp. 13–32). London: Falmer Press.

Office of the United Nations High Commission for Human Rights. (1989). Convention on the Rights of the Child. Retrieved February 22, 2010, from http://www2.ohchr.org/english/law/crc.htm

Oliver, J. E. (1993). Intergenerational transmission of child abuse: Rates, research, and clinical implications. *American Journal Psychiatry, 150*(9), 1315–1324.

Olwig, K. R. (1990). Designs upon children's special places. *Children's Environments Quarterly, 7*(4), 47–53.

Osler, A. (1998). Conflicts, controversy, and caring: Young people's attitudes towards children's rights. In C. Holden & N. Clough (Eds.), *Children as citizens: Education for participation* (pp. 113–126). London: Jessica Kingsley.

Peterson, R. (1992). *Life in a crowded place: Making a learning community.* Portsmouth, NH: Heinemann.

Pharr, S. (1988). *Homophobia: A weapon of sexism.* Little Rock, AR: Chardon Press.

Phillips, B., & Alderson, P. (2002) *Beyond 'anti-smacking': Challenging violence and coercion in parent–child relations.* London: The Children's Society.

Piaget, J. (1932). *The moral judgment of the child.* London: Kegan Paul, Trench, Trubner.

Piaget, J. (1959). *Judgment and reasoning in the child.* Paterson, NJ: Littlefield, Adams & Co.

Pufall, E., Rudkin, J. K., & Hall, E. (2004, June 3–5). Exploration of children's civil rights: Listening to the voices of children. Paper presented at the 34th annual meeting of the Piaget Society, Toronto.

Pugh, G., & Selleck, D. R. (1996). Listening to and communicating with young children. In R. Davie, G. Upton, & V. Varma (Eds.), *The voice of the child: A handbook for professionals* (pp. 120–136). London: Falmer Press.

Putnam, R. (1996, Winter). The strange disappearance of civic America. *American Prospect*, pp. 34–48.

Putnam, R. (2000). *Bowling alone: The collapse and revival of American community.* New York: Simon & Schuster.

Quann, V., & Wien, C. A. (2006). The visible empathy of infants and toddlers. *Young Children, 61*(4), 22–29.

Quortrup, J. (1987). Introduction: The sociology of childhood. *International Journal of Sociology, 17*(3), 3–37.

Reagon, B. (1991). *The songs are free* [Video recording]. New York: Mystic Fire Video.

Reagon, B. J. (1992). Coalition politics: Turning the century. In M. L. Anderson & P. H. Collins (Eds.), *Race, class, gender: An anthology* (pp. 503–509). Belmont, CA: Wadsworth. (Original work published 1981)

Reggio Children. (1995). *A journey into the rights of children.* Reggio Emilia, Italy: Author.

Rinaldi, C. (2001). Documentation and assessment: What is the relationship? In C. Guidici, C. Rinaldi, & M. Krechevsky (Eds.), *Making learning visible: Children as individual and group learners* (pp. 78–93). Reggio Emilia, Italy: Reggio Children.

Rinaldi, C. (2006). *In dialogue with Reggio Emilia: Listening, researching and learning.* London: Routledge.

Roche, J. (1996). Children's rights: A lawyer's view. In M. John (Ed.), *Children in our charge: The child's rights to resources* (pp. 23–35). London: Jessica Kingsley.

Roosevelt, E. (1953, March 27). Remarks at the United Nations. From Eleanor Roosevelt National Historic Site. Retrieved August 1, 2007, from http://www.nps.gov/archive/elro/who-is-er/er-quotes/

Rothenberg, J. J. (1994). Memories of schooling. *Teaching and Teacher Education, 10*(4), 369–379.

Rudkin, J. K. (2003). *Community psychology: Guiding principles and orienting concepts.* Upper Saddle Brook, NJ: Prentice Hall.

Rudkin, J. K., & Hall, E. (2005, June 9). Young children's rights, young children's voices. Poster session presented at the biennial meeting of the Society for Community Research and Social Action, Champaign, IL.

Ryan, W. (1971). *Blaming the victim.* New York: Vintage Books.

Schiavo, R. S. (1987). Home use and evaluation by suburban youth: Gender differences. *Children's Environment Quarterly, 4*(4), 8–11.

Schiavo, R. S. (1990). Children's and adolescents' designs of ideal homes. *Children's Environment Quarterly, 7*(2), 37–46.

Schiff, S. (2003, April 27). Because I said so. [Review of the book *Raising America* by A. Hulbert]. *New York Times,* p. 1. Retrieved July 10, 2007, from http://nytimes.com/2003/04/27/books/reviews/27SCHIFFT.html

Schneir, M. (Ed.). (1972). *Feminism: The essential historical writings.* New York: Vintage Books.

Sebba, R. (1991). The landscapes of childhood: The reflection of children's environment in adult memories and in children's attitudes. *Environment and Behavior, 23*(4), 395–422.

Shakespeare, T. (2001, February 16). Understanding disability. Keynote address at Disability with Attitude Conference, University of Western Sydney, Parramatta Campus Session. Retrieved March 14, 2005, from http://www.srdrn.unsw.edu.au/conferences/TShakespeare-keynote.DWA

Shamgar-Handleman, L. O., & Belkin, R. (1984). They won't stay home forever: Patterns of home space allocation. *Urban Anthropology, 13*(1), 117–144.

Shantz, C. U. (1987). Conflicts between children. *Child Development, 58,* 283–305.

Shapiro, J. P. (1993). A hidden army for civil rights. In *No pity: People with disabilities forging a new civil rights movement* (pp. 105–142). New York: Random House.

Siegel, M. (2005). *False alarm: The truth about the epidemic of fear.* Hoboken, NJ: Wiley.

Singer, E., & Hannikainen, M. (2002). The teachers' role in territorial conflicts. *Journal of Research in Early Childhood Education, 17*(1), 5–18.

Smith, A. B. (2002). Interpreting and supporting participation rights: Contributions from sociocultural theory. *The International Journal of Children's Rights, 10*, 73–88.

Smith, A. B., Gollop, M., Marshall, K., & Nairn, K. (Eds.). (2000). *Advocating for children: International perspectives on children's rights*. Dunedin, New Zealand: University of Otago Press.

Sobel, D. (1993). *Children's special places: Exploring the role of forts, dens, and bush houses in middle childhood*. Tucson, AZ: Zephyr Press.

Solomon, D., Watson, M. S., & Battistich, V. A. (2001). Teaching and schooling effects on moral/prosocial development. In V. Richardson (Ed.), *Handbook of research on teaching* (4th ed., pp. 566–603). Washington, DC: American Educational Research Association.

Sommer, D., Pramling Samuelsson, I., & Hundeide, K. (2010). *Child perspectives and children's perspectives in theory and practice*. New York: Springer.

Stanton, A., & Unkrich, L. (Co-directors). (2003). *Finding Nemo* [Motion picture]. United States: Disney-Pixar.

Stanton, E. C. (1889). *A history of woman suffrage* (Vol. 1, pp. 70–71). Rochester, NY: Fowler and Wells. Retrieved March 14, 2005, from http://www.fordham.edu/halsall/mod/Senecafalls.html

Sutton-Smith, B. (1990). School playground as festival. *Children's Environment Quarterly, 7*(2) 3–7.

Tognoli, J., & Horwitz, J. (1982). From childhood home to adult home: Environmental transformations. In P. Bart, A. Chen, & G. Francescato (Eds.), *Knowledge of design* (pp. 321–328). Washington, DC: Environmental Design Research Association.

Trimble, S. (1994). The scripture of maps, the names of trees: A child's landscape. In G. P. Nabhan & S. Trimble, *The geography of childhood: Why children need wild places* (pp. 17–31). Boston: Beacon Press.

Tuan, Y. (1977). *Space and place: The perspective of experience*. Minneapolis: University of Minnesota Press.

Turiel, E. (2002). *The culture of morality: Social development, context, and conflict*. Cambridge: University of Cambridge Press.

UNICEF. (n. d.). *Convention on the rights of the child*. Retrieved July 27, 2007, from http://www.unicef.org/crc/

U.S. Census Bureau. (2008). Retrieved January 25, 2010, from http://factfinder.census.gov/servlet/ACSSAFFFacts?_submenuId=factsheet_0&_sse=on

Vaish, A., Carpenter, M., & Tomasello, M. (2009). Sympathy through affective perspective taking and its relation to prosocial behavior in toddlers. *Developmental Psychology, 45*(2), 534–543

Vygotsky, L. S. (1978). *Mind and society: The development of higher mental processes*. Cambridge, MA: Harvard University Press.

Wagner, J. T. (2004, September). Fishing naked: Nordic early childhood philosophy, policy, and practice. *Young Children,* pp. 56–62.

Walker, N. E., Brooks, C. M., & Wrightsman, L. S. (1999). *Children's rights in the United States: In search of a national policy*. Thousand Oaks, CA: Sage.

Wenner, M. (2009). The serious need for play. *Scientific American Mind.* Retrieved January 17, 2010, from http://www.sciam.com/article.cfm?id=the-serious-need-for-play

Wiggin, K. (2003). *Children's rights: A book of nursery logic.* (Original work published 1892) Retrieved August 7, 2007, from http://www.gutenberg.org/catalog/world/readfile?fk_files=41765

Wolfe, M. (1978). Childhood and privacy. In I. Altman & J. Wohlwill (Eds.), *Human behaviour and the environment: Advances in theory and research: Vol. 3. Children and the environment* (pp. 175–222). New York & London: Plenum Press.

Woolf, V. (1991). *A room of one's own.* New York: Harcourt Brace Jovanovich. (Original work published 1929)

Wortman, C. B., & Lehman, D. R. (1985). Reactions to victims of life crises: Support attempts that fail. In I. G. Samson & B. R. Sarason (Eds.), *Social support: Theory, research and applications* (pp. 463–489). Dordrecht, The Netherlands: Martinus Nijhoff.

Yamamoto, K. (1979). *Children in time and space.* New York: Teachers College Press.

Zeegers, S. K., Readdick, C. A., & Hansen-Gandy, S. (1994). Daycare children's establishment of territory to experience privacy. *Children's Environments, 11*(4), 1–10.

Index

Abolitionist movement, 28–29
Abuse, 41–42
Adams, J., 37–38
Adams, M., 24
Adult social power, 22, 27, 55, 56–57
Alderson, Priscilla, 2, 10, 12, 17, 26, 37, 42, 46–47, 58, 114
Ali, Muhammad, 30
All About Love (hooks), 41
"All God's Children Got Shoes" (song), 26, 77
Altman, I., 105
Americans with Disabilities Act of 1990, 33
Ariès, Philippe, 48
Arrieta, Gabriela Azurduy, 34
Asch, A., 33
Assisted participation, 32
Assor, Avi, 41
Authoritarian parenting, 55–56
Authoritative parenting, 55–56
Autonomy, 32–33

Bandman, Bertram, 51
Bateson, Mary Catherine, 48
Battistich, V. A., 61
Baumrind, Diana, 55
Bayer, C. L., 59
Bedrooms, as children's places, 103, 105, 106, 111
Belkin, R., 95
Bell, L., 24
Bellah, R. N., 50
Belyea, M., 44
Berman, S., 53
Berra, Yogi, 23
Black civil rights movement, 24–28, 29, 30, 34
Blaming the Victim (Ryan), 43
Boulder Journey School
    Charter on Children's Rights, 7–19, 24, 32, 39, 51, 56, 57, 79, 99
    children's places project, 94, 97–107
    Crystal's City hamster project, 68–92
    described, 1
    Hurricane Katrina project, 63–65, 67
    image of the child and, 25–26
    materials to facilitate communication, 11–12
    moon buggy project, 61–62, 63, 64
    Saturn 5 project, 57–58, 59, 61
    setting for, 3
    as social context for children's communal responsibilities, 52–55
    supportive social learning and, 55
Bowlby, John, 41

Bridges, Ruby, 25
Brooks, C. M., 21
Brown, Linda, 25
Brown v. Board of Education, 25

Carpenter, M., 52
Challas, G., 41–42
Charter on Children's Rights, Boulder Journal School, 7–19, 24, 32, 39, 51, 56, 57, 79, 99
Cherney, I., 3
Cheynut, Audrey, 34
Childhood, as status, 48–49
Child promoting, 33–34, 84
Child proofing, 33–34, 84
Children's Crusade, 25
Children's places, 94–111
    adult memories of, 94, 107–108
    bedrooms, 103, 105, 106, 111
    Boulder Journey School project, 94, 97–107
    characteristics of, 96–107
    for children, 104–109
    children defining space for themselves, 97–100
    concept of place, 94–95
    Crystal's City and, 95–96, 99, 102
    drawings and photographs, 98, 100, 102–106, 110, 111
    in England, 100–101
    forts, 94–96
    marginalized position of children and, 95, 107
    natural spaces, 98–99
    privacy and, 95–96, 104–107
    rules for, 105–107
    in Sweden, 38, 100, 105
    thresholds and boundaries in, 100–104, 107, 108
Children's rights, 36–49
    adult/child developmental differences, 42–45
    adult/child life experience differences, 45–46
    adult/child relationships of "loving interdependence," 47–48, 114
    Boulder Journal School Charter on Children's Rights, 7–19, 24, 32, 39, 51, 56, 57, 79, 99
    children's insights into, 17–18
    commitment to, 3
    in context of community participation, 50–55
    in different countries, 21, 36–38, 100, 105
    images of children and, 113–114
    nature of, 114
    peer relationships and, 114
    protection versus participation in, 18, 21, 37–40, 82–86
    questions surrounding, 112–113

Children's rights, *continued*
    unique status of children, 40–48
    United Nations Convention on the Rights of
        Children (UNCRC), 2, 20–21, 36–37, 50, 66, 95,
        114
    in the United States, 21
    universal nature of childhood, 41–42
Civil rights, 21, 24–28, 29, 30, 34
Clark, Alison, 10, 95
Clarkson, Elizabeth, 68–92
Cobb, E., 100
Codependency, 43
Collectivism, 16–17, 52
Community participation, 2, 50–67
    adult role in supporting children, 55–58
    conflict and, 58–62
    in global and local communities, 62–65
    rights and responsibilities in context of, 50–55
    right to community, 86–91, 92
    social context for, 52–55
Conditional love, 41
Cone, J., 25, 47
Conflict, 58–62
    cultural differences in, 60
    rules and, 61–62
Convergent thinking, 44–45
Corporal punishment, 31
Covell, K., 50
Creativity, in listening to young children, 10–12
Crystal's City hamster project, 68–92
    balancing protection and participation, 82–86
    children's places and, 95–96, 99, 102
    design and development, 68–74
    drawings, 70, 71, 74, 78, 81, 82, 83, 86, 87, 88, 90
    foam core, 71–73, 75, 76
    importance of movement, 74–82
    inside versus outside Crystal's City project, 84–86
    right to community, 86–91, 92
    successor hamsters, 94

Dahlberg, Gunilla, 63
Damon, William, 52, 54–55, 59, 62, 109
Da Ros, D. A., 60
Dawe, H. C., 59
Deci, E., 41
Declaration of Independence, 28
Declaration of Sentiments, 28–29
de Coninck-Smith, N., 95
Democracy, 29, 30
Denmark, 21
Developmental differences, 42–45
Dewey, John, 2, 53
Dialectics of Sex (Firestone), 31
Disability rights movement, 31–34
Divergent thinking, 44–45
Doherty-Sneddon, G., 10
Douglass, Frederick, 28, 29
Dovey, K., 94, 99, 103
Drawings
    children's places and, 98, 100, 102–106, 110, 111
    in Crystal's City hamster project, 70, 71, 74, 78, 81,
        82, 83, 86, 87, 88, 90
    in making meaning for children, 64

Eastenson, A., 60
Edwards, Carolyn, 1–2, 45, 52, 62
Egocentrism, 91
Eibl-Eibesfeldt, Irenaus, 54
Eisenberg, N., 52
Elections Canada, 50–51
Elkind, D., 36–37, 40, 42–43, 47
Ellison, Ralph, 23
Emotional responsiveness, 52
Empathy, 52
England, 100–101
Erikson, Erik, 109
Etzioni, Amitai, 50

Family
    hamster city project and, 87–89, 92
    parenting styles, 55–56
    as social context for children's communal
        responsibilities, 52
Farson, Richard, 36–37, 40, 42
Feminine Mystique (Friedan), 29
Feussner, J. R., 44
Finding Nemo (movie), 38–39
Fine, M., 33
Firestone, Shulamith, 31
Forman, G., 1–2, 45
Fraser, S., 56
Freire, Paulo, 23, 27, 48
Freud, S., 91
Friedan, Betty, 29–30

Gandini, L., 1–2, 45
Gans, R., 53
Gardner, Howard, 99
Garrison, William Lloyd, 28
Geography of Childhood, The (Nabhan), 98
Gestwicki, C., 56
Giese, N., 44
Gilligan, Carol, 33
Gini, Al, 22
Glass, T. A., 44
Glassner, B., 37
Golding, William, 111
Goldschmeid, E., 33
Gollop, M., 66
Gossip, 43
Greenman, James, 38, 40, 95
Griffin, P., 24
Gutman, M., 95

Hall, Ellen, 7, 44, 55
Hamster city project. *See* Crystal's City hamster
    project
Hannikainen, M., 59, 60
Hansen-Gandy, S., 94, 96, 105
Harding, Vincent, 24–25, 27–28, 35
Harris, Judith Rich, 54–55, 110
Hart, Roger, 10, 47, 49, 97, 107
Hart, S., 3, 54
Hartig, T., 94
Hartup, W. W., 59, 60
Hawkins, David, 48
"Heaven, Heaven" (song), 26

Hendricks, Audrey Faye, 25
Here and now, in listening to young children, 13–16
Heywood, C., 48
Hillman, I., 7
Hillman, M., 37–38
Hodson, V. K., 54
Hoffman, M. L., 52
hooks, bell, 41, 43
Horwitz, J., 95
Howe, R. B., 50
Human becomings/beings, 2–3
Human rights, 21
Humiliation, 55
Hundeide, K., 3
Hundred languages of children (Malaguzzi), 1, 3, 10, 45
Hurricane Katrina project, 63–65, 67
Hurried Child, The (Elkind), 36, 42, 47

Independent living, 32, 33
Individualism, 16–17, 32, 44, 52
Inherent vulnerability, 32
Invisibility, 23–24
Invisible Man (Ellison), 23

Jackson, S., 33
Jagow, A., 97, 104
Japan, 60
Johnson, H. B., 23
Johnson, Jack, 30
Jones, A., 26
Jones, E., 12
Jones, James, 23

Kagan, J., 26
Keller, Helen, 37
Kielburger, Craig, 50–51
Killen, M., 60
King, Billie Jean, 30
King, Martin Luther, Jr., 25, 47, 79, 115
Kjørholt, A. T., 56–57
Kleinman, Shirley, 44
Kohlberg, Lawrence, 33
Kohn, Alfie, 24, 41, 53–54
Korczak, Janus, 42
Korpela, K., 94
Kovach, B. A., 60
Kylin, Maria, 95, 100, 103, 107
Kytta, M., 94

Ladder of Young People's Participation/Student
    Involvement in School (Hart), 47, 49
Langsted, O., 10, 13, 14, 21, 54, 58
Lansdown, G., 32, 37, 50, 53
Laursen, B., 59, 60
Lehman, D. R., 44
Levine, E., 25
Lewis, C. C., 60
Liberation theory, 40, 47–48
Life experience, 45–46
Listening to young children, 10–17
    collective and individual voices, 16–17
    creativity in, 10–12

here and now in, 13–16
    hundred languages of children (Malaguzzi), 1, 3, 10, 45
    "mosaic" approach to, 10, 95
    patience in, 12–13
    pedagogy of listening, 2
Lorde, Audre, 35
Lord of the Flies (Golding), 111
Louis, Joe, 30
Louv, Richard, 38, 99, 100
Love
    conditional, 41
    through indulgence, 48
    relationship of loving interdependence, 47–48, 114
    transformative energy of, 92

Madsen, R., 50
Maher, A., 57
Malaguzzi, Loris, 1, 45, 52
Malcolm X, 25, 47
Mandenko, 60
Marginalized groups, 34, 43, 95, 107. *See also* Oppression
Margulis, S. T., 104
Marshall, K., 66
Maruyama, M., 60
Matchar, D. B., 44
May, S. E., 59
Mayall, Barry, 16, 43, 114
Mayer, R. H., 25
McKay, F., 60
McLeod, A., 10
McLerran, A., 94
Mead, Margaret, 54
Mealtime, 14–15
Melton, G. B., 3, 114
Memmi, Albert, 23
Menn, L., 44
Miljeteig, P., 10
Miller, Alice, 41
Miller, D. L., 41–42
Montessori, Maria, 33, 43, 79
Moon buggy project, 61–62, 63, 64
Mooney, C. G., 33
Moore, Robin C., 54, 97, 104
Mooreshead, A., 38
Moral development, 54–55, 59
Moral reasoning, 32–33
Moss, Peter, 10, 22, 38, 42, 47, 62, 63, 95, 109
Moyers, Bill, 26–27
Municipality of Reggio Emilia Infant Toddler Centers
    and Preschools, 1

Nabhan, Gary P., 12, 38, 99
Nairn, K., 66
Narcissitic infant, 91
Natural spaces, as children's places, 98–99
Navajo, 60
Nebelong, H., 37
Nutbrown, C., 51

Oakley, A., 16, 29, 31

Office of the United Nations High Commission for Human Rights, 36–37, 95
O'Keefe, Georgia, 3, 91
Oliver, J. E., 42
Olwig, K. R., 97
Oppression, 23–34, 43
    Black civil rights movement, 24–28, 29, 30, 34
    disability rights movement, 31–34
    requirements of, 43
    second women's movement, 28–31
Osler, A., 3
Overprotection, 38–39

Painting, in making meaning for children, 64
Parents
    parenting styles, 55–56
    in Saturn 5 project, 57–58, 59, 61
Participation rights, 18, 21, 25, 32, 37–38, 82–86, 95
Patience, in listening to young children, 12–13
Pavlovic, Z., 3
Pedagogy of listening, 2
Peers
    children's rights and, 114
    importance in developing communal responsibilities, 54–55
Pence, E., 63
Permissive parenting, 55–56
Permissive teaching, 55–56
Perry, N. W., 3
Peterson, R., 103
Petrie, P., 22, 38, 42, 47, 62, 109
Pharr, S., 23
Phillips, B., 42
Physical disabilities, 23
Piaget, Jean, 54, 59, 91
Places of children. *See* Children's places
Play, 38, 40
    conflict in, 59–62
    importance of, 12
Power
    accountability for use of, 46
    adult social power, 22, 27, 55, 56–57
    based on age, 42, 45–46, 48
Praise, 42
Pramling Samuelsson, I., 3
Privacy, children's places and, 95–96, 104–107
Prosocial behavior, 52
Protection rights, 18, 25, 37–40, 82–86
Psychosocial development, 16–17
Pufall, E., 7
Pugh, G., 2, 10, 11
Punishment, 56
Putnam, Robert, 50

Quann, V., 52
Quortrup, J., 42

Readdick, C. A., 94, 96, 105
Reagon, Bernice Johnson, 26–27, 109–110
Rebecca of Sunnybrook Farm (Wiggin), 48
Reggio Children, 45, 59
Reggio Emilia approach, 1, 25–26, 33, 45
Reproductive freedom, 31
Reynolds, G., 12

Riggs, Bobby, 30
Rights of children. *See* Children's rights
Riihela, Monika, 9
Rinaldi, Carlina, 2, 10, 44, 48
Roche, Jeremy, 22
Rockwell, Norman, 25
Room of One's One, A (Woolf), 95, 98–99
Roosevelt, Eleanor, 21
Rose, Nikolas, 22
Roth, G., 41
Rothenberg, J. J., 55
Roxaboxen (McLerran), 94
Rudkin, J. K., 7, 25, 55
Rules
    children's places and, 105–107
    conflict and, 61–62
Ryan, William, 23, 43

Safety, 38–39
Saturn 5 project, 57–58, 59, 61
Schiavo, R. S., 95, 103
Schiff, S., 13
Schneir, M., 29
School
    decision-making by children in, 53–54
    as social context for children's communal responsibilities, 52–54
Sebba, R., 99
Second women's movement, 28–31
Self-centeredness, 52
Self-determination, 32–33, 36, 50–51, 81–82
Self-expression, 17–18, 50–51
Self-interest, 50–51
Self-regulation, 56
Self-sufficiency, 33
Selleck, D. R., 2, 10, 11
Seneca Falls Conference (1848), 28–30
Separate but equal, 29
Shakespeare, Tom, 32
Shakespeare, William, 95
Shamgar-Handleman, L. O., 95
Shantz, C. U., 60
Shapiro, Joseph P., 23
Siegel, M., 37
Sieminski, J., 57
Singer, E., 59, 60
Slavery, 28–29
Smith, Anne B., 58, 66
Sobel, David, 96, 98, 103–104
Social context
    adult roles in, 55–58
    children as protagonists, 55–58, 62–65
    for children's communal responsibilities, 52–55
    global and local communities, 62–65
    peer learning in, 54–55
    valuing conflict in, 58–62
Social statuses, 41–42
Solomon, D., 61
Sommer, D., 3
Spaces of children. *See* Children's places
Speed Racer (cartoon), 30–31
Stanton, Elizabeth Cady, 28–29
Stewart, H. L., 60
Structural changes in the environment, 33–34

Structural vulnerability, 32
Suffrage movement, 28–29
Sullivan, W. M., 50
Supportive social learning, 55
Sutton-Smith, Brian, 12, 111
Sweden, 38, 100, 106
Sweet Honey in the Rock, 27
Swidler, A., 50

Teachers
    adult social power and, 22, 27, 55, 56–57
    conflict among children and, 61
    supportive social learning and, 56
    teaching styles, 55–56
"This Little Light of Mine" (song), 20, 26–27
Tipton, S. M., 50
Tognoli, J., 95
Tomasello, M., 52
Touch, 46
Trimble, S., 12, 38, 97
Truth, Sojourner, 28
Tuan, Yi-Fu, 94
Turiel, Eliot, 52, 60

Unconditional Parenting (Kohn), 24
UNICEF, 2, 58
UNICEF Canada, 50–51
United Nations Convention on the Rights of Children
    (UNCRC), 2, 20–21, 36–37, 50, 66, 95, 114
United Nations High Commission on Human Rights,
    21
U.S. Census Bureau, 3

Vaish, A., 52
Voice of young children
    listening to, 10–17
    voicelessness, 23–24
Vygotsky, Lev S., 16–17, 58

Wacky Races (cartoon), 30
Wagner, J. T., 111
Walker, N. E., 21
Watson, M. S., 61
Wenner, M., 12
Whaley, K. L., 59
Whitelegg, J., 37–38
Wien, C. A., 52
Wiggin, Kate Douglas, 48

Wolfe, M., 104, 107
Women's movement, 28–31
Woolf, Virginia, 95, 98–100
Words, in making meaning for children, 63
Wortman, C. B., 44
Wrightsman, L. S., 21

Yamamoto, K., 95
Young, D., 104–105

Zeegers, S. K., 94, 96, 106
Zeidner, M., 3
Zone of proximal development (ZPD; Vygotsky),
    16–17, 58

About the Authors

Ellen Lynn Hall, proud mother of three children and grandmother of four, is Executive Director of Boulder Journey School, a school of 250 young children, their families, and a faculty of 50 educators. Ellen is an adjunct faculty member at the University of Colorado Denver. She created and directs the Boulder Journey School Teacher Education Program, in partnership with the University of Colorado Denver, which offers a teaching license in Early Childhood Education and master's degree in Early Childhood Education or Educational Psychology. She is also Vice President of Videatives, a Web-based company that offers resources for teacher educators and educational consultants. Ellen received her doctoral degree in educational leadership and innovation from the University of Colorado Denver, her master's degree in deaf education from Smith College, and her bachelor's degree in mathematics from the University of Massachusetts Amherst. Ellen's research focuses on early childhood education, specifically the rights of children, exemplified in the schools for young children in Reggio Emilia, Italy, and in the work of world-renowned educators David and Frances Hawkins. She is a founding board member of Hawkins Centers of Learning and the North America Reggio Emilia Alliance. Publications on the rights of children include: "Giving Value to the Rights of Children: Questions for Consideration by a School Community," *Exchange,* May/June 2009, and "Supportive Social Learning: Creating Classroom Communities That Care," *Childcare Information Exchange,* January/February 2003, with Jennifer Kofkin Rudkin. Ellen has presented work on children's rights through the World Forum on Early Care and Education in Acapulco, Mexico (2003), Kuala Lumpur, Malaysia (2007), and Belfast, Ireland (2009). Ellen is a member of the World Forum Foundation International Organizing Committee.

Jennifer Kofkin Rudkin received a Ph.D. in community psychology from the University of Virginia and completed postdoctoral training in child development at the University of Denver. She has taught in traditional and nontraditional universities, including the University of Denver, Union Institute, and The Evergreen State College. She also has conducted basic and applied research in academic, government, and nonprofit settings. Her research, teaching, and writing have centered on the importance of attending to the voices of disenfranchised people. She wrote an influential textbook entitled *Community Psychology: Guiding Principles and Orienting Concepts,* and currently teaches in the School of Education at University of Colorado Denver. She lives with her partner and two children and also works as a professional artist.